It's Time to Talk to Your Kids About Porn

It's Time to Talk to Your Kids About Porn

A Parent's Guide to Helping Children and Teens Develop Sexual Integrity

Greta Eskridge

NELSON
BOOKS

An Imprint of Thomas Nelson

Published in Nashville, Tennessee, by Nelson Books, an imprint of Thomas Nelson. Nelson Books and Thomas Nelson are registered trademarks of HarperCollins Christian Publishing, Inc.

Author is represented by Jenni Burke of Illuminate Literary Agency, www.illluminateliterary.com.

Thomas Nelson titles may be purchased in bulk for educational, business, fundraising, or sales promotional use. For information, please email SpecialMarkets@ThomasNelson.com.

Scripture quotations are taken from The Holy Bible, New International Version®, NIV®. Copyright © 1973, 1978, 1984, 2011 by Biblica, Inc.® Used by permission of Zondervan. All rights reserved worldwide. www.Zondervan.com. The "NIV" and "New International Version" are trademarks registered in the United States Patent and Trademark Office by Biblica, Inc.®

Any internet addresses, phone numbers, or company or product information printed in this book are offered as a resource and are not intended in any way to be or to imply an endorsement by Thomas Nelson, nor does Thomas Nelson vouch for the existence, content, or services of these sites, phone numbers, companies, or products beyond the life of this book.

The advice and strategies presented in this book are intended as general guidance and may not be suitable for every family or situation. This book should not be considered a substitute for professional advice or consultation with qualified experts. Readers are encouraged to use their discretion and seek appropriate professional support when necessary.

Library of Congress Cataloging-in-Publication Data

Names: Eskridge, Greta, 1976- author.
Title: It's time to talk to your kids about porn : a parent's guide to helping children and teens
    develop sexual integrity / Greta Eskridge.
Description: Nashville, Tennessee : Nelson Books, [2025] | Includes bibliographical references.
    | Summary: "Author, speaker, and mom of four, Greta Eskridge equips parents to have
    age-appropriate, honest, and hope-filled conversations about pornography with kids of
    any age so that they can help their children develop lifelong sexual integrity"--Provided by
    publisher.
Identifiers: LCCN 2024041334 (print) | ISBN 9781400250608 (trade paperback) | ISBN
    9781400250240 (ebook)
Subjects: LCSH: Children and pornography. | Sex instruction for children--Religious aspects--
    Christianity. | Children--Sexual behavior. | Parenting--Religious aspects--Christianity.
Classification: LCC HQ784.S45 E85 2025 (print) | LCC HQ784.S45 (ebook) | DDC
    649/.65--dc23/eng/20241014
LC record available at https://lccn.loc.gov/2024041334
LC ebook record available at https://lccn.loc.gov/2024041335

For Aaron
For our children
For the men, women, and children who have
been hurt or victimized by pornography
There is hope, there is healing, and there is
something so much better waiting for you.
"And I will restore to you the years that
the locust hath eaten." (Joel 2:25)

Contents

CONTENTS

PART THREE: THE HARDEST QUESTIONS

Foreword

We haven't always had to worry so much about childhood slipping away too soon. There was a time when society had built-in safeguards that preserved the innocence of kids. Cartoons had their limits—they aired at set times and then disappeared from view. Television shows were tethered to the living room, unable to follow us wherever we went. The neighborhood was a sanctuary, where children played freely outside, their laughter carried by the breeze. College applications and résumé-building were distant concerns, reserved for the far-off days of older adolescence. Even the darker things, like pornography, were hidden away in magazines, difficult to find and usually far removed from everyday life.

Slowly, over the past several decades, the foundations that once shielded childhood have eroded. Guardrails that protected our youth have been dismantled, piece by piece. The small shifts seemed subtle, but they added up to create a tsunami of challenges for children in their growing-up years. The rise of relentless academic pressures, the shrinking of recess time, and the astronomical increase in screen usage have all taken their toll. And the once-unimaginable ease with which children now access pornography—a far more extreme and destructive form than past generations ever encountered—has become the stark reality. The age of exposure is no longer in the distant teenage years; it's happening now, in elementary schools, to kids as young as eight or nine.

These attacks on childhood are relentless, and the damage they inflict is often carried far beyond those early years. What once was a time of discovery and wonder is now too often marked by confusion, shame, and the weight of struggles too heavy for young shoulders to bear.

But as the storm grows, here stands Greta Eskridge: a beacon of hope for parents navigating these uncharted waters. Greta has never been one to turn away from hard truths. Instead, she steps into the fray, armed with knowledge, compassion, and a deep belief that parents are still the most powerful force in their children's lives. She knows, as all great guides do, that it's not too late to rebuild the defenses that protect our kids. She brings us back to the heart of what it means to be a parent, offering the tools, the words, and the wisdom we need to face this new reality with courage.

Greta's work is more than just a guide; it's a lifeline for families caught in the currents of a world that often feels out of control. As a mother of four—with one already an adult—Greta has walked this path before us. She understands the fears and challenges we face because she has lived them herself. Through her practical advice, her depth of understanding, and her unwavering commitment to truth, she calls us back to the front lines of parenting. She reminds us that it's not the schools, the screens, or the society at large that will protect our kids—it's us. And in these pages, she shows us how.

Greta, with her genuine warmth, her infectious energy, and her sharp mind, has a way of making even the toughest conversations feel possible. She tackles the topic of pornography with grace and wisdom, giving parents the language they need to address this sensitive issue head-on. She helps us understand that we are in a day and age when silence is no longer an option. Through open, honest, and loving dialogue, we can equip our children to navigate a world full of dangers without losing their innocence or their joy.

Thank you, Greta, for leading the charge in this battle for our children's hearts and minds. Your work is a gift to parents everywhere, offering not just hope but a clear path forward. In a time when so much feels uncertain, you remind us that there is still power in the parent-child relationship, and that with the right tools we can help our kids grow up healthy, whole, and unafraid.

Ginny Yurich
Founder of 1000 Hours Outside

A Letter to Parents

Dear friends,

I am so glad you had the courage to pick this book up. I mean, who wants to read a book about porn? Almost no one. Most people shy away from the topic of pornography altogether—especially when it comes to their kids. But you showed up! And that speaks volumes about your willingness to step into hard places for the sake of protecting your kids.

The truth is, pornography brings up a lot. For many of us, it triggers feelings of shame, fear, awkwardness, hurt, anger, trauma, sorrow, frustration, embarrassment, and more. You might be struggling with some of those feelings right now. I want you to know that it is okay if you are hurting, frustrated, sorrowful, or even angry because of the way pornography has impacted your life. I stand with you. I know those feelings too. And I encourage you to hold on to these words that comforted me on my darkest days: "Of one thing I am perfectly sure: God's story never ends with 'ashes.'"[1]

I also want you to know that if you or your spouse have engaged with pornography, that doesn't mean you can never talk to your kids about it. There is hope! Your story might be what God uses to help save your children from the dark things you're dealing with. That's been true in our family, and it can be for yours too.

This book won't cover all the newest things happening in the online world: AI, the latest apps, what memes and slang are trending, and all the rest. From the time I write the manuscript to the time this book gets into your hands, those things will have changed. Instead, I'm going to coach you in how to talk to your kids about pornography, sex, and all kinds of other challenging topics. Because the most important thing you can do to help your kids is to simply *talk to them about it all*. Having open communication with you about pornography is their best defense and their best chance for recovery after they've been exposed to it.

It's my prayer that you will finish this book knowing you don't have to be defeated by pornography. We serve a God who is mightier than the strongest darkness, and He is with us in this fight. I love this quote by Betsie ten Boom, made famous by her sister, the incredible Corrie ten Boom: "There is no pit so deep that God's love is not deeper still."[2] Yes, even the pit of pornography.

Remember these words Jesus spoke in John 10:10: "The thief comes only to steal and kill and destroy; I have come that they may have life, and have it to the full." Jesus came that we might have a full, abundant life. Yes, even an abundant sexual life, which is the complete opposite of cheap, counterfeit pornography. Through freedom in Christ, we have so much to offer our children!

Before we fully dive in, I'd like to offer a prayer for you to use as you move forward:

Lord, please give me courage.
Give me courage to begin healing where there is hurt.
Give me courage to reject shame in myself and others.
Give me courage to begin speaking when I have no words.
Lord, please give me hope.
Give me hope when I am afraid.
Give me hope when I am overwhelmed by sadness.
Give me hope when I am angry.
Lord, please be with me on this journey.
Amen.

Let's get started,
Greta

PART ONE

Why You Need to Talk to Your Kids About Porn

ONE

Why I Became an Unlikely Porn Fighter

Pornography is a heavy and difficult subject. It is layered in shame, trauma, fear, embarrassment, disgust, anger, and more. These feelings have kept people silent about pornography for generations. You might be struggling with some of these feelings right now. Maybe they've kept you silent even though you know you need to talk to your kids.

Parents, if you want a guide to navigate these rough waters, I'm here to be that guide! I know I'm "just a mom." But I'm also a mama bear, here to protect my kids and help you protect yours. Who fights harder to keep her cubs safe than a mama bear? I'm willing to do whatever it takes to give our kids a safe and healthy sexual future, something pornography is trying to steal from them. But we must speak up! It's time to break the silence and dare to do something different.

It's hard to do. I get it. I grew up in a traditional Christian home, and while my parents did a fantastic job providing me with a safe and beautiful childhood, we didn't really talk about sex. As far as sexual things go—good or bad—I was very sheltered. And pornography was so far off my radar that I don't even remember hearing the word until I was in my late teens. It just wasn't something we talked about or something I had to deal with. Of course, those were the olden days when porn wasn't accessible at any moment of the day on a device that fits in a back pocket. In those days a person had to work hard to find pornography. I didn't look for it, and it never came looking for me. And even though my parents gave me only the most simple and basic info about pornography and seldom mentioned it again, I was fortunate to never be exposed to it as a child or teen.

I am grateful for my innocent childhood. It was a gift not everyone is granted. That is part of the reason I'm fighting for our kids now. They deserve the best we can give them, despite the world they are growing up in. We just can't afford to say nothing or next to nothing and trust that our kids probably won't discover pornography or be exposed to it by a pop-up ad, another kid in their class, or a stranger on Snapchat.

According to one source "the average age of first exposure" is twelve, and 93 percent of boys and 63 percent of girls are exposed by age eighteen.[1] Hearing this should make us all the more willing to step into the ring and fight for our kids.

Still, you might find yourself wondering, *How can I possibly talk to my kids about pornography? I was stressing about telling them the truth about the tooth fairy. And won't it steal the innocence of their childhood?* I felt the same way the first time I had to talk to my sons about pornography and protecting their bodies from anyone who tried to touch them inappropriately. I hated bringing up the idea that there were people who might want to hurt them online or in real life. Telling this to my sons made me sick to my stomach. Their world was so safe and beautiful. By suggesting someone could hurt them, I felt like I was stealing some of that beauty from them.

But by saying nothing I would be leaving them open to the possibility of ugliness and darkness being brought into their lives. I once received a message from a reader that exemplifies this:

> As a social worker I've experienced firsthand what not speaking up does to a child's mind, varying from mild depression to straight-up suicide attempts. By speaking up you're protecting them not only from pornography but also from the large-scale effects of it on their developing brains and personalities.

I had to decide between shining a light into the darkness or letting the darkness invade. I chose to shine the light into a dark place. This is the decision we face when talking to our kids about pornography. I appreciate the words of Martin Daubney, former editor of *Loaded* magazine and now a public advocate for protecting kids from porn:

> Like many parents I fear my boy's childhood could be taken away by pornography. So we have to fight back. We need to get tech-savvy, and as toe curling as it seems, we are the first generation that will have to talk to our children about porn. . . . By talking to them, they stand a chance. If we stick our heads in the sand, we are fooling only ourselves.[2]

I deeply resonate with that resistance to having the "toe curling" conversation. For much of my life I could hardly utter the word "pornography" aloud, let alone have a conversation about it. But that unwillingness to bring up an uncomfortable subject didn't help me. In fact, it was part of my greatest pain.

MY STORY

My husband, Aaron, and I had been married for about twelve years. We had three young children, and our life was full and happy. It was kind of crazy, of course, with three kids under age four, but we loved them all so much it helped make up for the chaos. Around this time I began to notice new behaviors in Aaron. He seemed to be withdrawing from me, from our friends, and from church activities. He became quick to explode with anger, he was always stressed, and he was often unable to sleep.

Because of my lack of knowledge regarding pornography, I didn't know that these could be signs of a porn addiction. Changes in personality, intense anger, self-loathing, anxiety, depression, or even suicidal thoughts can be hints that someone is struggling with heavy porn use or addiction. I didn't know any of this, and so I blamed him for his problems. As far as I could see, our life was perfect: three healthy kids, a home, a good job, and friends and family we loved. What did he have to be angry and stressed about?

Aaron asked if we could go to counseling. It was his cry for help, and I didn't listen. I suggested he go on his own, feeling sure that his problems weren't my issue. I was so wrong.

Eventually, Aaron's addiction contributed to him having an affair. It's common for men and women who engage in regular pornography use to want to engage in illicit behavior beyond what they're seeing on-screen. It is also common for them to experience dissatisfaction with their partner and to be more open to the idea of cheating. One study showed that regular pornography use increases the likelihood of infidelity by 300 percent.[3]

When Aaron confessed to the affair, it was one of the worst days of my life. The next came a few days later when I learned about his porn addiction. I would never have imagined that my beloved Aaron would use porn. In my mind, pornography users were creeps—not stable, married fathers who went to church, held down jobs, and took care of their families. Obviously, I was wrong.

At first I was in shock. But then the pieces of the puzzle began to come together, and I realized those nagging feelings I'd ignored had been trying to tell me something. Avoiding conversations I'd been afraid to have also helped us get to this place. It would have been so much better to face my fears and have the conversations with him, terrifying as they might have been.

Of course, I was not at fault for Aaron's use of pornography or his affair. But what if I had been willing to ask why? "Why do you think we need counseling?" "Why are you asking for help?" At the beginning it always feels easier to avoid the difficult conversations, but avoidance rarely leads to a good outcome. Aaron's confessions brought me face-to-face with this truth, and that was the moment I decided to stop avoiding and start being brave.

A PAINFUL EDUCATION

To help Aaron and myself heal, I had to learn all I could about this evil beast called pornography. I still loved Aaron. I believed in the man he was and could be again. I believed in his repentance and his desire to change. But I had to understand how pornography had ensnared him and almost destroyed our marriage. As we both pursued healing—together and separately—I found myself needing to know how pornography had gained such a powerful hold on him.

I began to read all I could find on the impact of pornography on the brain and heart of the consumer. I looked for personal stories shared on blogs. I looked for medical research and articles by psychologists. Part of my mission was to understand what my husband had been through. But I was also on a mission to protect our kids.

At this point we had four: three sons and one daughter. They were all still so young and innocent. I could not bear the idea of any of our sons using pornography, objectifying women, and one day breaking the heart of their wife. I couldn't bear the idea of my daughter watching pornography and believing she deserved to be used and abused like an object instead of a person. I promised myself I would do all in my power to provide something better for our kids. It became a part of my healing journey.

At first I kept the new things I was learning to myself. Aaron and I talked about it, but I wasn't out pounding the pavement and talking about pornography with perfect strangers the way I do now. I wasn't healed enough for that yet. Pornography was still an awkward, uncomfortable, and now incredibly painful topic. But I started to realize that none of my friends were talking about this. They were just as unwilling as I was to enter the conversation.

If I wanted change, if I wanted something better for my kids, then I needed to create a community of moms who'd be just as willing as I was to say, "We're going to do phones and technology and social media and all the rest in a totally different way than what culture is telling us to do. We are going to pursue face-to-face interactions and cultivate real relationships. We're going to have uncomfortable conversations so our kids know what pornography is and know why and how to turn away from it. We're going to build a better future. We're going to fight for our kids!"

The only problem was, I didn't know how to bring the subject up. But God did. That summer we attended a weeklong family camp at Forest Home in the San Bernardino Mountains of Southern California. Forest Home is like summer camp for kids, but the whole family gets to go. We sleep together in a cabin, eat together in the dining hall, and spend free time swimming in the lake, ziplining, or playing cards in the clubhouse. It's a blast! And every night while the kids have their own fun programming, we parents get to listen to fantastic speakers and learn from them.

The speaker that week was Josh McDowell. He surprised everyone that first night when he told us, "This week we are going to talk about pornography. I believe it's the greatest danger facing modern Christians. It is time for us to break the silence, or we'll never change anything." The discomfort in the room was palpable. I understood. My own eyes immediately filled with tears. Did I really want to spend a week talking about a topic that had caused so much pain in my life, in Aaron's life, and in our marriage?

Aaron squeezed my hand and whispered, "Are you going to be alright?"

I nodded. I was. I knew it was no accident that we were there and Josh was speaking on this topic. This was going to be a part of our healing process. It would be hard, and probably painful, but it would be worth it.

Some people, though, were more than surprised. They were unhappy or even angry that our speaker was going to be covering that topic. I heard someone say, "I came here to relax and have a good time. Not to get pounded over the head about something like the dangers of pornography."

Josh shared facts, statistics, and stories, and he gave us the truth about how pornography destroys people who use it—and often the people they love. His words hurt, but they also healed. My compassion for Aaron, who had been held in the suffocating grip of porn addiction, grew. His understanding of the pain he caused me also grew as Josh was quick to point out how an addict's actions impact their partner.

One night Josh shared an incredibly vulnerable part of his story. He told us how as a young boy he had been shown pornography and then been sexually molested by one of the men who worked on his father's farm. He shared that his parents didn't do anything to stop it because no one wanted to talk about such things. He shared about the years of hurt and trauma he endured because of these events and then the healing that God did in his heart, even giving him the grace to forgive. It was a powerful testimony to not only the damage pornography can cause but also the redemption that God can provide.

Josh bravely shared his story because he wanted to invite people to make a change and break the silence around pornography. So often effecting change means standing up and leading the way. Josh led, and I was ready to follow. His words lit a fire in me. I knew I wanted to do something. I knew I needed to do something. But I didn't know exactly what to do or where to start.

I spoke to Josh about it, briefly telling him my story. He listened intently, and when I was done he said, "Can you share that with moms? Can you offer them ways to help their kids? They need help. They need someone to show them how to talk about pornography in a healing way. They need to hear from a fellow mom. Will you do it?"

I smiled and said I would. I had my mission.

IT'S TIME TO REFLECT

- What has your experience with pornography been like?
- How does that experience make you feel about broaching the topic with your children?
- What feelings does reading my story or Josh's story bring up for you?
- If you are feeling things like shame, sadness, fear, or anger, who can you reach out to now to help you talk through those feelings and begin to heal?
- What element of hope are you holding on to after reading this chapter?

TWO

Why Moms Need to Break the Silence

When we got home from camp, I had the easiest intro ever to bringing up pornography even though I hadn't known how and was too scared to do so myself. Everyone asked, "How was camp?"

And I answered, "It was amazing! We had the most incredible speaker. He shared about the need to talk to our kids about the dangers of pornography and how we can do it. I learned so much." Then I proceeded to share what I'd learned. I was doing it! I was breaking the silence. It's true some listeners had nervous and uncomfortable looks on their faces. But they were listening. They didn't shut me out. Maybe people were willing to talk about pornography after all.

It wasn't time to tell our personal story with pornography because we were very much in the middle of healing. It was right for us to hold our story close and share it with just a few people who were walking with us as we continued that healing process. But I did want to share something. All my reading and learning and then hearing from Josh had spurred me on. I knew I could take what I'd learned and use it to help families protect their kids. I wanted to share with a bigger audience than just my friend circle.

Knowing how tender the topic still was for both of us, I asked Aaron what he thought about this idea. My plan was to open parents' eyes to the devastation pornography causes and then educate and empower them to help their kids. I'd be sharing as a concerned mom, not as the wife hurt by porn.

"I don't think I'm ready to share that part of our story yet," I told him. "But I believe doing this other thing will be part of my own healing. I'll be seeing good come from the pain. It feels like redemption. And I know parents out there need help. What do you think?"

Aaron's a good man. He didn't hesitate. "I think you should. It will help others, and I think it will help you."

A LIFE-CHANGING PODCAST EPISODE

I began to formulate a plan. I had a parenting podcast called *At Home* that I hosted with a few friends. That seemed a logical place to start sharing with invested parents. I told my cohosts, "I think we need to do an episode on pornography." They were not enthusiastic. It wasn't because they didn't think it mattered, but they felt uncomfortable talking about it.

I understood. Most moms I knew were not comfortable talking about pornography with their kids. More than one mom said to me, "Oh, my husband will talk to our sons about that. I don't need to be involved."

Of course, that response brought up a lot of questions from me:

But what if he doesn't talk to your sons? Will you?
Who is going to talk to your daughters? Your husband? You?
Don't you think your children could benefit from hearing your perspective as a woman about the danger and damage of pornography?
Don't you want your sons and your daughters to know women can speak out against porn just like men can?
Don't you agree that pornography is not just a male issue but one that impacts both men and women, therefore making it a human issue?

These questions were often met with an awkward silence. Again, I understood. Like me, many of these women had been raised in an era when we were told that porn was a man's issue. The fathers talked to the sons about it, and moms and daughters had no part in it. And even though pornography use by men most definitely impacted women, we weren't invited to be part of the conversation. There was almost no mention of girls or women who struggled with pornography use. People acted like this couldn't even happen. This outdated and misguided mindset of "pornography is a man's issue" lingered, leaving women without a voice in the conversation.

I knew moms needed to be equipped to talk to their kids about pornography, too, so I didn't give up on the idea. "I'll do the whole thing," I promised my friends. "You guys don't have to do a thing but be there for moral support." They agreed. I will never forget recording that podcast episode. I was very nervous. I had written out the entire show, everything I'd say word for word. We never did that for podcast episodes because they were usually a conversation between the four of us, very informal and unscripted. This was different because I'd be the only one talking. It would also be the first time I'd spoken publicly about a topic that felt tender, raw, awkward, and uncomfortable.

My friends and I gathered around the table for the podcast, prayed together, and hit Record. For some reason two of our mics weren't working. So my three friends crowded around a mic at one end of the table with me at the other. "We might decide to say something," they told me. "So we'll just share this mic." But as I began to talk, all I remember is their eyes widening with each new thing I shared, and they didn't say a word.

My voice shook when I started. It was a good thing I was sitting down because I'm sure my knees would have been knocking together. My armpits were sweaty, and my mouth was dry. I awkwardly shared what parents need to know about pornography: "Studies have found that frequency of porn use correlates with depression, anxiety, stress, and social problems."[1] I explained that porn addiction can cause everything from brain damage to violent behavior to suicidal thoughts. Pornography is linked to child exploitation, sex trafficking, and sexual violence. It's dangerous and should be viewed as such.

I made sure, though, not to leave things there—healing and hope were part of the story too! One of the best ways to protect kids was to break the silence and start talking. I shared simple ways parents could begin those conversations with their kids and reminded them that this wasn't just about protecting kids now when they were young, middle schoolers, or even teens. It's about having a bigger vision, a long-term vision. We want to set our kids up for a *lifetime* of sexual wholeness and sexual integrity. What we do now matters. But this conversation isn't just about today. It isn't just about the next couple of years. It's about helping our kids for the rest of their lives!

ENTHUSIASTIC RESPONSE

The response to that podcast episode was overwhelming. The emails and comments on social media began to pour in. Some were reflective.

I encountered porn when I was in middle school and spent all of high school filled with shame and regret from my porn addiction. It still haunts me to this day, but I'm working on talking about it with kids. I carry so much shame from my own story with porn, but I feel the call to fight for their lives.

My father was addicted to porn from a young age and into his adult life. I believe his addiction led to his unfaithfulness to my mother and he left our family when I was sixteen. Now with three children of my own, and a faithful husband who loves the Lord and has done all he can to safeguard himself against the temptation, I have resolved to raise and guide my children to be informed and to protect their hearts and minds from the evils of pornography.

I grew up mostly in a legalistic, very sheltered, tight-lipped home and church. Unfortunately, a lot of terrible things happened to my siblings and me at the hands of "trusted friends." I was three years old—yes, *three*—the first time I was shown porn.

At first I took the sheltering, "don't share anything so they keep all their innocence" approach with my own kids. But I quickly realized it's not a matter of *if* but *when* they would be faced with these hard things I so wanted to keep them from. Thanks to your boldness to share these tips here, my husband and I have been able to have great conversations with our older three kids and feel they are much more prepared to face these circumstances than we were.

Some were grateful.

I wish we weren't so afraid to talk about this topic. Thank you for being bold!

I've wanted to talk to my kids about this but had no idea where to begin. Now I do!

This conversation is so needed, but I don't hear anyone talking about it. I'm so glad you are.

Some were educational.

My husband is a counselor, and he sees people all the time who were exposed to porn at a young age . . . and it literally rocks their world and ultimately affects marriages and parenting. All this could change if we had more parents openly talking about it with their children, as well as keeping those relational circuits open and strong (and accepting and not shaming). If kids were embraced and loved and helped through this, they wouldn't be needing to see my husband.

My husband and I used to pastor young adults. The devastation we've seen from porn addiction has been awful. We even walked alongside one of our young men as he confessed to assault and did prison time. A large part of his story was a deep porn addiction that began at age ten.

We just took in a foster son. His dad watched porn with him at the age of four. He's five now, and we are having constant problems with him being inappropriate with adults and kids, and he had to be removed from his three-year-old sister. Porn has broken his little brain. Praying for God to deliver him and heal him. Keep teaching what you are. The effects of porn are devastating.

Some were personal.

Pornography has impacted my marriage, and I wish with every part of my heart to fight and protect my children from lifelong addiction.

Some were holding on to the hope I offered.

You made us more aware and gave me both plenty of food for thought as well as things we should be doing as parents while also sharing that we have hope!

By then it was clear to me that parents, especially moms, weren't opposed to talking to their kids about pornography. Or listening to me talk about it. But they wanted guidance resources, help, and hope. They wanted someone on their team. I was ready to step up and be that person.

I closed that podcast episode by sharing a quote from the book *Christy* by Catherine Marshall. It encapsulates why I chose to talk about pornography:

> You see, evil is real—and powerful. It has to be fought, not explained away, not fled. And God is against evil all the way. So each of us has to decide where we stand, how we're going to live our lives. We can try to persuade ourselves that evil doesn't exist; live for ourselves and wink at evil. We can say it isn't so bad after all, maybe even try to call it fun by clothing it in silks and velvets. We can compromise with it, keep quiet about it and say it's none of our business. Or we can work on God's side, listen for His orders on strategy against the evil, no matter how horrible it is, and know that He can transform it.[2]

I stumbled upon that quote a month before I hosted that podcast. It brought tears to my eyes, and I knew it was not an accident that I'd found it. This quote is an invitation. How will you respond to the issue of pornography? You can hide from it and pretend it isn't really happening. You can say it isn't *that* bad. Or you can break the silence and watch God transform evil into good. That day I chose to speak up. Because every parent—dads *and* moms—needs to talk to their kids about pornography. Will you?

IT'S TIME TO REFLECT

- How were sex and related topics handled in the home you grew up in? How did it impact you as a child, teen, and now as an adult? Think of things you'd do the same and things you'd do differently with your family now.

- How do you feel about talking to your kids about pornography?
- If you feel something beyond the natural feelings of awkwardness, like real fear or shame, where do you think those feelings are coming from? How can you deal with them in a helpful way that leads to healing?
- As a mom, do you feel empowered or uncomfortable in the role of talking to your kids about pornography? Why? If you feel uncomfortable, begin to think of things that will empower you to step into this conversation with your children.

THREE

Why Your Kids Need to Hear You Talk About Porn

I was twenty-two years old when I began teaching high school. I was fresh from college and ready to make a difference in the lives of my students. Since I had been homeschooled for nearly my entire education, it was my first time in a public high school. And though I'd spent the last five years in a public university, some things about life on a public high school campus shocked me. The day I saw one of my ninth-grade students with a sexually explicit picture proudly displayed in his binder was one of those days.

Some teachers would have walked right by and not even noticed that picture of a woman's nearly naked rear end. She wore a G-string bikini, but honestly it was hard to see any string. It was an extremely sexual picture and wildly inappropriate to be carrying around school. But even more disturbing was what else the picture depicted. A man's hand held a large, heavy frying pan as if ready to hit her rear end with it. Neither the woman nor the man's face was shown—just her butt and his strong arm ready to inflict physical harm on her.

I was shocked. And in the way of a new, idealistic teacher, I called my student out on it with the hopes of making a difference. After saying I needed to talk to him for a minute, we stepped into the hallway, which was blissfully quiet while everyone else was in class. I took a deep breath and said, "Hey, you can't have that picture on your binder when you're in my classroom. You probably aren't allowed to have it in school at all."

I'm not sure he even knew what I was talking about because his initial response was anger that I dared tell him his personal property wasn't allowed in my classroom. "You can't tell me what I can have in my binder," he said indignantly.

That's when I got more specific. "Do you know this photo is demeaning to me and every other female student in our classroom? Do you know it's offensive and it objectifies women?"

At this point my student was genuinely baffled. He had no idea what I was talking about. Thankfully I realized I was coming on way too strong and reacting out of my own frustration and distress over that image. So I slowed down.

"Do you know what 'objectification' means?"

He shook his head no.

"Do you know what 'demeaning' means?"

Again, he shook his head.

I tried to explain as gently and succinctly as possible. "'Objectification' means you turn a person into an object. They aren't human anymore with a brain and thoughts and emotions and feelings. They are just a thing. Like the woman in the picture doesn't have a face or a body. She is nothing but her almost-naked bottom. When a person is objectified, it is easier to use and abuse them because you don't see them as fully human. You don't have to respect them or treat them well."

He looked at me like he kind of, maybe barely understood what I meant.

I kept trying. "And when I say that picture is demeaning to me, to your female classmates, and to any other female who sees it, what I mean is it's not respectful toward women. It doesn't honor her and so it doesn't honor us."

He looked at me with genuine confusion. "But it's just a picture."

"True. But that is a real woman who took that picture. And she is someone's daughter or sister or friend or maybe mom. And whether you know it or not, looking at pictures like this begins to train your brain to see women as objects. So, yes, it is just a picture. But looking at it can have real consequences. That is why I wanted to talk to you about it. I care about you. I care about how you view women now and in your future. I care about the girls in my classroom. I want what is best for all of you. And this picture in your binder does not represent what is best for any of us."

I went on to tell him that pictures like this that seemed funny or cool or harmless could be a gateway to much more destructive and dangerous images, and I cared too much about him to not say anything.

I'm fairly certain he thought I was crazy. The bewilderment he felt at our conversation was evident. So I asked him, "Has anyone ever talked to you about these things before?"

"No!" he answered emphatically.

"Well, as awkward as this feels for both of us," I told him, "I hope you remember the words of your weird ninth-grade

English teacher, and that you become a respecter of women and not a user."

He nodded and we went back inside. When the bell rang and I dismissed the class, he walked up to my desk and handed me the picture, clearly torn from the inside of a magazine. I would like to tell you he handed me that picture with conviction and pride that he was doing the right thing. Instead, he still looked irritated and embarrassed about the whole thing.

The rest of the school year went by with no more incidents or talks between the two of us, and all I can do is hope that my well-meaning message hung around in his head over the years and helped him consider a different way of doing things. If no one else was going to tell him the uncomfortable truth, I'm glad I was able to.

This experience, and others like it, had a profound impact on me. I did not yet have children of my own, but it made me wonder, *How can I protect the children I hope to have one day from this kind of sexual experience? How can I teach my sons that women are not objects and should be seen and celebrated as whole people? How should I teach my daughters that they are so much more than their sexual body parts?* I knew even then that this was going to be a battle. I just didn't know how big of a battle or all that it would cost until years later.

PARENTAL PUSHBACK

When my podcast team released that first episode on the subject of talking to kids about pornography, the responses came pouring in. Parents wanted to talk about this topic! They needed to. Many were wanting help and guidance with this challenging subject. Others had heavy stories to share and nowhere they felt safe sharing. I quickly found myself overwhelmed by the weight of these stories. This was the cost of stepping into the battle, one I couldn't have imagined that day when I was a high school teacher holding the story of my student. He was just one story, and now I felt the weight of holding many. Most of them contained a lot of hurt and trauma.

There were messages from parents who felt compelled by the episode to check their children's phones or devices and then found porn. They were saddened, angry, or scared and at a loss for what to do next. There were messages from college girls who shared they were addicted to pornography, and many of their friends were too. They felt so alone in their struggle. There were marriages damaged or even broken by porn.

My heart broke whenever I heard any of these stories but especially those from wives, because I knew their pain so intimately. One message from a wife asked me to pray for her husband. He served in law enforcement and investigated child pornography. I could not imagine what horrors he'd witnessed to protect those vulnerable children from further harm. It was so much to take in.

In the face of such evil, it's tempting to give in to despair and become paralyzed by it. This was one of the moments where I had to again decide whether I would shine light in a dark place or let the darkness invade. I chose to keep shining.

The way forward was to keep learning, keep researching, and most of all keep sharing with other parents. Because if I had ever felt paralyzed by fear and despair, they did too. All the messages made it abundantly clear: Parents knew they needed to talk to their kids about pornography, but most had no idea how. That was when I started writing and speaking on this. It was scary and I didn't particularly love doing it. I asked God why He hadn't given me a more fun topic to share with the world. But it was abundantly clear that this was the path marked out for me.

Even with so many parents responding positively, there was still plenty of pushback. It wasn't that parents didn't believe porn was evil and kids needed protection from it. It was more that they didn't think *their* kids needed protection from it. I heard the same reasons again and again.

Reason 1: My kids are too young.

While this may have been true in the past when porn wasn't accessible via technology, it just isn't anymore. We have all seen three-year-olds sitting in the cart at Costco, swiping away on their mama's phone while she shops. We all know unsupervised six-year-olds are playing games on an iPad or tablet. And since ten is the average age for kids in America to get their own smartphone, every single one of those kids is at risk of accidentally stumbling across porn. In fact, children under ten account for 22 percent of online porn consumption for those under eighteen.[1]

So even if you have every security measure enabled on your devices and you're using the strongest protection software and router, there isn't 100 percent protection from porn for any of us. Even our kids. Once while I was researching a hike on Google, I clicked on a link for info. It was not a pop-up ad but an actual link at the top of my search. Up popped a picture of naked women.

I was so unprepared and shocked that I gasped and turned

my phone over. I wanted to hide it. And then I couldn't get them off the screen! It took turning off my phone to get the image to disappear. How did this glitch happen? I have no idea. I have every security restriction enabled. In fact, I have to enter a password just to look at my own website because of the articles I have posted there about pornography. Yet somehow that image got through.

Our children are just as susceptible to this kind of scenario as we are. No one is too young to stumble upon pornography. No one is immune. So while we'd like to believe our kids are too young to need a conversation about pornography, if your child is over six years old, you need to talk to them.

Reason 2: My kids don't know about sex yet.

Here is an important truth for you to hang on to: Your kids don't have to know all about sex for you to warn them about pornography. Yes, that's right! Depending on their age, you don't have to tell them all the details for them to know porn is bad and dangerous. Instead, you only need to give them the minimal information necessary to keep them safe. All they need to know is that pornography is pictures and movies of people with no clothes on, and that it's not good for them, so you're doing your job and keeping them safe from it.

When they are young, they do not need to know anything explicit about the sexual aspect of pornography. Just tell them the most basic facts, enough for their protection, and leave it at that. As they grow, you can reveal more as it is needed. But if your kids don't know the details about sex yet, don't let that stop you from protecting them from porn by explaining, with the simplest details, how they can stay away from it.

Reason 3: My kids will become curious about porn.

Most people are curious about sex and sexuality because God created us to be sexual beings. Being curious about sex does not make your child bad. Being curious about porn does not make your child bad.

What would be bad is you not talking to your kids about sex or porn so that when their curiosity grows, they seek out answers on Google. And Google becomes their teacher instead of you. Or they accidentally stumble upon porn for the first time, and their curiosity drives them back for more. But they don't know if they should talk to you about it because you never said anything to them about porn.

We don't refuse to warn our kids about the dangers of crossing the street alone, touching a hot stove, smoking or doing drugs, or drinking and driving just because they might be curious to try those things after we bring them up. No! We recognize those activities are dangerous and offer appropriate warnings. Our approach toward pornography should be exactly the same. Porn is just as dangerous as those other activities.

The reality is your kid might become curious about porn after you warn them about it. But that is not a good reason to avoid talking to them. Instead, make sure your conversation covers what to do if they see porn, whether by accident or because they searched it out. Be certain they know to come to you, and that you will not love them less or heap shame upon them if they've seen porn. Make sure they know they are safe with you. And when they do come, respond with compassion and grace.

TALKING TO YOUR KIDS FOR THE FIRST TIME ABOUT PORNOGRAPHY

AGES 6 TO 8

Key concept

Pornography is pictures and movies of people with no clothes on. Looking at those is not good for you, so I'm doing my job to help keep you safe from it.

Also see the script "Talking to Your Kids After Pornography Exposure" in chapter 11.

THE HEART OF THE MATTER

I know that talking to your kids about pornography is not easy at any age. After all, we bring our own fears, hurts, shame, and other baggage to these discussions. But we can't let that stop us from offering our kids the protection they deserve. Remember there is a spiritual aspect to this fight.

That's the heart of the matter. It's not the porn industry tricking us and lying to us, but the father of lies himself. First Peter 5:8 describes him as a roaring lion, prowling around and looking for someone to devour. Satan wants to use porn to attack individuals, marriages, families, and even children. When we stand against pornography, we are fighting against a darkness and an evil that is bigger than just that industry.

We can't leave out this part of the fight. As parents we need to be educating and equipping them, but we must also pray for them. Prayer is our best defense against pornography because it invites in the One who loves our children even more than we do, and He promises to meet us with grace. "Let us then approach God's throne of grace with confidence, so that we may receive mercy and find grace to help us in our time of need" (Hebrews 4:16).

THERE IS ALWAYS HOPE

So what can we do? First, we must remember that we are not without hope. We serve a mighty God, and His light is brighter than any darkness. But that doesn't mean we can just sit by and hope for the best. We need to take action. I am fighting for open and honest conversations about these topics. Not just with my own kids but with other parents, with you, so you can talk to your kids too. We all have to work together to protect our kids and give them something better than the empty, sad, and dangerous future that porn is offering. Remember, *by doing and saying nothing, you are not helping your child.* In fact, you are doing just the opposite. I think this anonymous quote says it so well: "The only thing necessary for evil to triumph is for good men to do nothing."

Doing something is always hard, but it's always worth it. When I'm tempted to take a step back, I'm reminded of the messages I've gotten from parents over the years and I'm encouraged to keep going. Here's one example:

> Because of your bravery and passion for sharing about how
> to talk with your children about pornography, we've seen a

generational curse lift in our family. I'm a mama of three sons and I've been so fearful of how to help them guard their eyes and hearts ... your resources, candor, and consistency in sharing has empowered and equipped my husband and I to have some of the best talks in our life with our kids and to help them see the beauty of sex and how God designs our body within its original and perfect context.

Twenty-six years later, I still think about that ninth grader and our conversation in the school hallway. I'm grateful that our interactions pushed me to have that first awkward-but-so-important conversation. Because of that boy, I learned that showing up and showing another way of doing things mattered more than saying it perfectly. If we as parents aren't willing to face our fears and push through the awkwardness, to call out what is evil and talk to our kids about porn, we're just leaving them as prey to the wolves. Will it be hard? Probably yes. Will it be worth it? Most assuredly yes!

Consider this my invitation to join a troop of parents who know why they need to talk to their kids about porn and are ready to learn how to do it. We aren't alone, and together we *can* change the world for our kids and their kids and their kids.

IT'S TIME TO REFLECT

- How would you have responded to that ninth grader?
- How would you respond to your child in a similar situation?
- If you feel paralyzed by the idea of talking to your child about something like the ninth-grader's photo, think of

three things you could say in that moment and practice saying them.

- Which of the reasons parents often give for not talking to their kids about porn do you most relate to? Why do you think that is? How has this chapter helped you address that concern?

- If you have a story of sexual brokenness—either your own, in your marriage, or your child's—do you have a safe person or place to share that? If not, can you identify one now or begin to look for that person in your life?

FOUR

Why You Need to Parent from a Place of Hope

One of my first thoughts after learning of Aaron's affair and porn addiction was, *I don't want this for our kids, and I will do whatever it takes to save them from it.* I didn't want our kids to be exposed to pornography, to become addicted, to endure the suffering that porn addiction causes, and to inflict suffering on their future spouses and families. I was terrified at the thought of one of our kids dating and marrying someone who used porn—or even worse had an addiction and would walk the same road we'd been down. It became a mission, bordering on obsession, to protect them from the hurt Aaron and I had gone through. And for a time I really believed that by doing all the right things I had the power to save our kids from the heartache pornography brings.

My thoughts and actions were entirely understandable given my situation. But they led me to parent from a place of fear. I truly believed I could bubble wrap our kids, hide them from all the technology, keep the evil internet away at all costs, and that doing this would save them. I learned so much about pornography that I walked the line of becoming overprotective due to my fear.

Some parents respond to the issues of tech and porn like I did, but others deal with it by avoiding it altogether. For a variety of reasons, they find it easier to never learn or talk about it. I understand that. Neither of these extreme approaches are ideal, but they make sense. When we experience trauma we can have a multitude of reactions. Then it's easy to take our experiences and parent out of that trauma. In our minds, we have knowledge and experience that give us insight others can't understand when they haven't walked our journey. They don't know the risks and the hurt. Therefore, we believe we must build a hedge of protection around our kids because no one can protect them the way we can.

Friends, I know this feels true, *but it isn't*. I'm reminded of the verse from Psalm 20:7: "Some trust in chariots and some in horses, but we trust in the name of the LORD our God." Whatever your chariot or horse is, if that is where you are putting your trust, it is misplaced. Because it is not the chariot, the horse, the parental controls, the tech rules, the limited internet access, or even a ban of all tech and screens that will keep your kids safe. It is the Lord our God. He is the One who we place our trust and faith in.

It took me time and healing to come to this understanding. When I was first thrown into that place of brokenness, I didn't even know about trauma or how to heal from it. I just responded the best way I knew how, which was to circle up my wagons and protect my family from the hurt I now knew pornography could inflict. In time I began to use my hurt to help others.

My responses were noble and beautiful aspirations, but they were also too much for me to hold. I wish I could go back and tell that hurt and brokenhearted version of me, "You can't save them. But God can. You don't need to put that pressure on yourself. It's too much for you to carry. Give it to Jesus. He promises to carry our burdens. You can't prevent your kids from seeing porn or being hurt by porn. But that doesn't mean you are without hope. There is so much you can do."

Whatever you're working though when it comes to the difficult topic of pornography, I hope you'll understand there is no such thing as "porn-proofing" your kid. That doesn't mean you have to parent from a place of paralysis, despair, avoidance, or fear. We can't ignore the fact that our kids are growing up in a world where they are facing things we never had to deal with as children. It's our responsibility to give them the tools they need to stay safe online: how to respond to predators, interact with media wisely, practice discernment, be aware of the digital footprint they're creating, listen to their intuition, and so much more. Whether your child has access to screens at age five or fifteen, they need to learn these things!

Not giving your kids any access to technology isn't a realistic long-term solution, as much as I wanted to do this early on my journey. You can and should definitely give them the gift of a childhood untethered to screens. But there will come a time when they have to start using technology.

BEST PRACTICES FOR TECH USE

When I became a mom of teens, I came face-to-face with the fact that they would have to use technology. But there was a time when I never imagined I'd get to this place. I really believed we'd be tech free till they were eighteen. Again, this was parenting out of a place of trauma and fear by trying to keep the highest walls of protection around my kids for as long as possible.

When my kids were all young, we limited most tech access. We didn't have a TV or cable. There were no tablets, iPads, or video games of any kind in our home. I had a flip phone until my oldest was nearly ten years old, and even when I got a smartphone, my kids were not using it to play games, access apps, or text friends. They got to watch preapproved TV shows on our laptop that Aaron or I set up for them. They also listened together to preselected audiobooks on my phone.

This limited access to tech was a way we provided that protection we so desperately wanted for our kids. It was doable and sustainable when they were all young. And it was a tremendous gift to them! It offered them a low-tech childhood. In their most formative years they were learning to be entertained by something other than a screen. They were learning to use tech safely and wisely with support from their parents.

I firmly believe in introducing technology as slowly as possible when our kids are young. But that does not have to mean no exposure at all—it means limiting exposure while teaching them how to use it wisely.

Our kids need minimal interactions with screens until the age of ten, eleven, or twelve years old. If they are on screens for school, then they certainly should use them less when at home.

Yes, this will mean more work for you because you can't rely on screens and tech to entertain them or keep them busy. Instead, you'll need to teach them how to play, create, be entertained by books, use their imaginations, make messes, and even tolerate boredom.

1. Parental controls

As soon as your kids start engaging with screens, usually by preschool age, it is time to begin putting safety measures in place, like installing a router in your home. Routers help prevent dangerous and inappropriate content from getting onto your devices through the Wi-Fi. You should enable all the parental controls on tablets, phones, computers, smart TVs, and gaming systems.

For example, at a young age your child does not need the password to your phone or computer. They still need to ask permission to access these devices, because in the early years they still need your protection before gaining access. By the time they are in the teen years, giving them access shows that you have nothing to hide. These are ways of engaging with tech and screens that are safety forward and not fear based.

2. Safe search practices

Teach safe search practices. When younger children want to know something, the first person they should ask is you, not Google. Be their Google! Establish a routine where if a child wants to watch a show, look at the Lego website, or find a drawing tutorial, they come to you, explain what they want to do, and ask for your help. You sit with them and help them look up what they want to see. This establishes that access to the digital world is not to be done in private but out in the open. While a child is online, watching a show, or however they are using a device, they should be out in the open—in the kitchen with you while you wash dishes, in the living room where everyone is passing through—not in their bedroom alone and more vulnerable to making bad decisions.

3. Conversations about tech use

When our kids became teens I realized I needed to make adjustments to the way I handled technology. My teens were going to have to use tech and screens—for work, for school projects, for scouting, for driving, for communicating with friends and family, and yes, even for entertainment. Therefore, it was my job to help them learn to use it well, use it safely, and use it wisely.

I also realized more fully that conversation is the number one tool in keeping kids safe online. This is why I advocate so hard for parents to *talk* to their kids and not merely set rules and say something like, "Porn is bad. Don't use it." The truth is, we can have all the rules we want, but once our kids set foot outside our home, our rules don't matter anymore. Because all the other kids with phones might not have the same rules we do. And routers, software, and parental controls are important, but if your kids can't talk to you when those things fail, then all the safeguards mean nothing.

Instead, we must have conversations on safe and discerning tech use, screen addiction, gaming, social media, and pornography. We have to reach our kids' hearts. We have to help them see that porn is a dangerous, destructive lie. We have to help them see there is something better for them. This comes through honest, open, continuous conversation. And through this we create a culture in which our kids know they can come to us with questions, concerns, confessions, and all the problems they're facing. Conversation is key.

IT IS A BIG DEAL

Society, and really the people producing pornography, want us to believe that pornography is no big deal. They want you to believe kids seeing porn is nothing more than harmless fun and normal curiosity. They'd have us believe it can even be a healthy way to learn about sex. But this point of view could not be more wrong! Dr. Jill Manning says that children and adolescents are considered the most vulnerable audience of sexually explicit material because they "have limited ability to emotionally, cognitively, and physiologically process obscene material they encounter voluntarily or involuntarily."[1] Here are some of the ways a child, tween, or teen can be victimized by viewing and consuming pornography:

Trauma: Whatever age a child is exposed to pornography, the graphic and violent nature can be traumatic. Symptoms of experiencing this trauma can include things like shame, fear, and a negative view of sex.

Premature Sexual Awakening: First-time exposure to pornography for a child is often accidental and unintentional. If that child isn't given the opportunity to process the exposure, he or she might be prematurely sexually awakened and curious about sexual things before they are developmentally ready.

Unrealistic Expectations: A child is unable to discern that nothing about pornography is real. This can lead them to having unrealistic expectations about sex and dissatisfaction in their future sexual relationships.

Promiscuity: Pornography normalizes and promotes promiscuity as desirable behavior. This can encourage the viewer to engage in promiscuous behavior and can also increase the chance of marital unfaithfulness.

Body Dissatisfaction: Body dissatisfaction and poor self-image are common outcomes for both boys and girls who consume pornography. This dissatisfaction can be directed at themselves or their sexual partners.

Objectification: Pornography objectifies people, which can cause those consuming it to view people as objects for their own use and pleasure. This can negatively impact relationships, both sexual and nonsexual.

Normalizing Sexual Violence: Because of the violent nature of most pornography being produced now, both boys and girls can have a dangerously distorted view of sex. Boys may believe they should treat their sexual partners with violence, and girls may believe they should expect to be treated violently.

Addiction: Due to the extremely addictive nature of pornography, especially on a developing brain, a child or adolescent who regularly consumes porn is susceptible to porn addiction. This can lead them to engage in risky behavior and experience depression, shame, self-hatred, and even suicidal ideation.

I know these truths are heavy. I hope this information will encourage you to start those hard conversations and help your kids develop sexual integrity and discernment as they interact with the world. I believe we can become the generation of parents who says, "We will no longer be silent. We will rise up against this evil scourge of pornography and raise children who do not delight in evil but rejoice with the truth!" (1 Corinthians 13:6).

HOW TO PRAY AGAINST PORN

It is imperative we remember the spiritual aspect to this fight. Satan wants to attack our children. We are fighting against a darkness and an evil that is bigger than the pornography industry. This is rooted in the very forces of Satan himself. This verse from Ephesians 6:12 says it so well: "For our struggle is not against flesh and blood, but against the rulers, against the authorities, against the powers of this dark world and against the spiritual forces of evil in the heavenly realms." Knowing this, we must practice praying for our children and their protection from pornography and from the evil one.

Here are topics surrounding pornography that you can pray for your children through their childhood and into adulthood.

> Pray for Protection: Pray for protection from porn exposure, from enticement to return to porn, from sexual predators, and from addiction.
> Pray for Openness to Conversation: Pray for a willingness to engage in conversations about safe tech use and the dangers of pornography.
> Pray for Discernment: Pray that your children will be wise consumers of media and have the discernment to reject anyone or anything trying to manipulate or deceive them.

Pray for Strength to Reject Pornography: Pray that they will be steadfast to resist the temptation to view and use pornography.

Pray for Courage in Confession: Pray they will have the courage to confess to you or others if they are struggling with pornography use. Pray also that they will be a person of safety, compassion, and help if they have a friend who confesses to them.

Pray for Compassion in Discovery: Pray that you will respond with grace and compassion upon discovery of porn use. Pray also that you will be led to helpful resources for their healing.

Pray for Boldness in Speaking Against Porn: Pray they would be a bold voice in sharing the harms of pornography and the freedom that comes from pursuing sexual health.

Pray for Generational Safety: Pray their future spouses, children, and grandchildren will be protected from the harmful impact of pornography.

Pray for Healing After Exposure to Pornography: Pray that God will remove the images they've seen from their minds and memories. Pray for the desire to return to pornography to dissipate. Pray for qualified and wise counselors to provide help and recovery. Pray for their brain to develop new coping skills and habits through neuroplasticity.

While we know our children will encounter pornography at some point, we pray they will have the strength to turn away when they do. There is no porn-proof bubble we can place them in, but we can give them the knowledge, tools, and convictions to stand firm in the fight. We don't want to send them into battle unequipped, so we train them, we talk to them, we support them, and we pray for them. We aren't parenting from a place of fear. Instead, we do all of this to give our kids, and their kids after them, a fighting chance against pornography. It is time to impact the future generations for good. It's time to parent with hope!

IT'S TIME TO REFLECT

- Are you parenting out of a place of fear and control or out of protection and hope?
- If you feel yourself fighting fear, consider memorizing this verse from Micah 7:7 and lean on this hope from God's Word when you are afraid: "But as for me, I watch in hope for the LORD, I wait for God my Savior; my God will hear me."
- Have you experienced any trauma that is leading you to parent out of fear and control? Who can you talk to about that trauma to begin seeking healing?
- What safe tech practices can you implement in your home and family right now? If you feel overwhelmed, choose just one thing from your list and make a plan for putting it into place this week.
- After reading the list of damage porn can cause to kids, what stood out to you the most?
- Choose one item from the prayer list and focus on praying that for your child or yourself this week.

FIVE

Why You Have to Learn to Discern

We live in a time when it's unpopular to believe in absolutes. People want to find loopholes and excuses and say, "Well, it's okay just in this instance." But we cannot back down from the truth that pornography is not good for anyone and especially could never be good for children.

Here are lies the pornography industry wants us to believe:

- Pornography is safe if there is consent.
- Pornography can be used for healthy sex education.
- Pornography is good as long as it doesn't involve violence.
- Pornography is ethical when those making it are getting paid "enough."

Porn is a gigantic business, and they want to keep making money. The industry's annual revenue is approximately $97 billion—more than the revenues of Microsoft, Google, Amazon, eBay, Yahoo, Earthlink, Apple, and Netflix combined.[1] When there is so much money to be made, porn producers will do whatever it takes to get anyone, even children, hooked on their product.

They're working hard to normalize and trivialize porn to the point that it is a regular and accepted part of culture. Some people call this living in a pornified culture. A common and seemingly harmless example of this is the hashtag #foodporn, which is used when people post a picture of their smoothie bowl or their Sunday brunch on social media. You'll also see the hashtag #bookshelfporn for pictures of beautifully styled book-shelves, or #cabinporn for pictures depicting gorgeous cabins in the forest or next to an alpine lake. Culture wants to desensitize us to pornography by making light of it. It's simple things like this that are so insidious. If adults don't realize they're being affected by the pornified culture around them, how much more unaware are our children?

A bolder example of this normalizing and trivializing of pornography happened in October 2020, when Kraft Mac & Cheese released a new ad campaign. Kraft promised to send a free box of their mac and cheese to a loved one of anyone who took a pic of their own mac and cheese and posted it with the hashtag #sendnoods. The ads featured pixilated, fuzzy pictures of bowls of mac and cheese, meant to remind viewers of an inappropriate picture that had to be blurred out. Kraft also said, "We know the best way to show your love is to send noods."[2]

A video ad featured *Saturday Night Live*'s Vanessa Bayer saying, "In these strange times, people are in need of extra comfort. That's why it's always a nice gesture to send noods so they know you're thinking of them. Noods, I mean. Not nudes."[3]

The correlation in this ad between "noods" and "nudes" is obvious. This was not an accident but a deliberate attempt to trivialize the use of porn and of sending nudes. Obviously this was an inappropriate choice for an ad campaign, but when you recognize that the target audience of Kraft Mac & Cheese is children, the campaign becomes disgusting and dangerous.

It was beyond irresponsible for Kraft to make this ad, and there was plenty of backlash. Kraft canceled the campaign within a week. But there were still plenty of people leaving them positive comments and sharing the ads and videos. Many people saw it all as a big joke and they loved it. This was especially true of the younger demographic, which aligns with a survey that asked a group of students aged thirteen to twenty-four which would bother them more, looking at porn or throwing their plastic water bottle in the trash instead of recycling.

The majority of students said it was more immoral to not recycle than it was to look at pornography.[4] In fact, 90 percent of teens and 96 percent of young adults are either encouraging, accepting, or neutral when they talk about porn with their friends.[5]

These numbers reflect kids who have grown up in a pornified culture that has told them over and over that porn is a normal, innocuous part of life. Everything they've been told and shown supports that porn is a joke to laugh at in TV shows, movies, and ad campaigns. It's no different from anything else you're obsessed with, like a good meal, a beautiful bookshelf, or a gorgeous cabin in the woods. And it's far less problematic than other issues like not recycling—which culture has told them is wrong since they were in preschool.

If you think pornography is wrong or dangerous, you could

be labeled as uptight, overly religious, or a prude. These are the messages our kids are being fed every single day via TV shows, movies, music, books, and hearing from their peers—especially on social media. We must help our kids learn to discern the truth from the lies.

Here are three ways to help your kids learn and practice discernment, even while growing up in a pornified culture.

1. CULTIVATE MEDIA LITERACY

One of the best ways we as parents can combat these lies culture is feeding our kids is to teach them to be discerning consumers of media. Media literacy means thinking critically about the media being consumed and analyzing it for hidden messages or agendas. I always told my kids that being media literate was like being a detective.

A great way to begin teaching this to your kids is by focusing on how all advertisers are trying to get us to feel something about a product so we'll want to purchase it. Watch some toy, cereal, or snack-food commercials. Ask your kids questions about the ads.

Continue to practice this in everyday life. You can point out ads on billboards while you drive, or at the movies before the show starts. Don't you always want a Coke and popcorn when they play that advertisement for concessions? Talk through the commercials that air when you're watching television or point out the print ads in magazines. Analyze the ads imbedded in websites. Advertising is everywhere, and the opportunities to critique are endless. Remember, the point is not to teach your kids to become cynical, judgmental people. It's to teach them to be critical thinkers and to practice discernment.

TALKING TO YOUR KIDS ABOUT MEDIA LITERACY

ALL AGES

Ask your kids questions as you interact with different forms of media. Here are a few springboard questions to get your conversation started.

1. Who made the ad?
2. Who is the ad targeted to?
3. What product is the ad selling?
4. Does the ad have a message?
5. Does the ad have a hidden or underlying message?
6. How does the ad make you feel?

2. IDENTIFY OBJECTIFICATION

The next step in training your kids to be discerning is to teach them to identify objectification: turning people into objects and stripping them of their humanity. Instead of seeing them as real people worthy of respect and honor, objectification means seeing them as things. We see this all the time in our culture—in movies, music videos, magazine covers, and even in comic books and cartoons. All of these are the training ground to desensitize us, and our kids, to objectification.

Pornography, of course, is the ultimate example of objectification. Pornography trains the brain to see humans as sexual objects to use and abuse for our own pleasure, and then to discard when they no longer satisfy us. That's why it's critical to teach our kids that human beings are worthy of respect and honor. We need to remind them often that their bodies, all bodies, are fearfully and wonderfully made in God's image. Calling out objectification as evil can be an aid in ultimately rejecting pornography.

After years of these conversations, my kids can easily identify examples of using sex to sell products. One time we were watching television at my parents' house, and a commercial came on for the snack cracker Triscuit. The commercial invited consumers to "Go toppingless!" and enjoy their crackers plain, without any toppings. My kids instantly spoke up: "Can you believe they're trying to use sex to sell a cracker?" "Yeah, of course they want you to think about the other kind of topless that has nothing to do with crackers."

Then we had a short conversation about how many people don't even realize they're being manipulated by commercials and advertisements because they just absorb it all without thinking about it. Once you've taught your kids to be media literate, they will be the ones leading the discussions. You just sit back and enjoy seeing them be critical thinkers who aren't mindlessly ingesting the toxic messages of our pornified culture. They have an opportunity to be a change agent in a world that wants to turn people into products.

TALKING TO YOUR KIDS ABOUT OBJECTIFICATION

Talking to your kids about objectification is necessary, but it doesn't have to be difficult. Here are some tips and concepts to help your conversations.

AGES 5 TO 10

Giving your kids a healthy view of their own body is the first step to help them see all humans as worthy of respect and honor. You can reinforce these ideas when you begin to talk about body safety. Seeing their own bodies as fearfully and wonderfully made will help kids understand that their bodies are worthy of respect, honor, and protection.

Key concept

Your body is an amazingly designed machine. Every part of your body is uniquely created for a specific purpose, and every part is wonderful!

Activity

Memorize Psalm 139:14: "I praise you because I am fearfully and wonderfully made; your works are wonderful, I know that full well."

Resource

A great book to aid you in this conversation is *God Made Me in His Image* by Justin and Lindsey Holcomb.

AGES 10 TO 12

When your child is around ten years old, you can introduce the concept of objectification without adding the sexual aspect. Use examples from history, books they've read, or in the media.

Key concept

Objectification is looking at and treating someone as an object instead of as a whole person. It's the opposite of respecting and honoring them the way God wants us to.

Activity

Memorize Philippians 2:3: "Do nothing out of selfish ambition or vain conceit. Rather, in humility value others above yourselves."

AGES 13+

For kids ages thirteen and up (or when your child is developmentally and emotionally ready), introduce the connection between sexually driven images and objectification. Helping them say no to porn consumption means addressing their heart, not just putting a parental block on their smartphone. Look for examples in movies, TV shows, music videos, advertisements, video games, on billboards and magazine covers, and even in comic books and cartoons. It will not take long for your kids to spot objectification happening all over the place.

Key concept

Objectification is looking at and treating someone as a sexual object instead of as a whole person. It is the opposite of respecting and honoring them the way God wants us to.

Pornography is the ultimate example of objectification. It teaches that people are products to be consumed, to be used, and often to be abused. This is why pornography is connected to sexual violence, sex trafficking, and even child pornography and child sexual abuse. It's also important to recognize that both men and women are objectified in pornography. Consuming it can change your view of people, making them appear less human.

Let's think of places we've seen objectification happen. Can you think of an example?

Activity

Memorize Romans 12:9–10: "Love must be sincere.

Hate what is evil; cling to what is good. . . . . Honor one another above yourselves."

Discussion Ideas

1. How can we change the narrative around objectification and not accept it as part of our own healthy sexual outlook?
2. What are ways we can practice viewing and treating fellow humans as whole people?
3. How can we honor and respect the human body in a world trying to make us do the opposite?

3. RECOGNIZE SOFT PORN

Another way to help our kids become discerning consumers of media is by teaching them how to identify soft porn and how it is used to grab their attention, hold it, and sell them a product. Many of us have become so desensitized to soft porn that we don't recognize the way it is seeping into our everyday life.

Think about how many video games have objectified and hypersexualized female characters. Or the way magazine covers featuring women wearing practically no clothing are displayed in stores at a child's eye level. TV shows and young adult romance novels contain steamy bedroom scenes. If we don't talk to our kids about what they're seeing, reading, and listening to, we're leaving them to believe these depicted behaviors and imagery are normal and acceptable.

Talking about soft porn instead of pretending it isn't there helps our kids understand that advertisers, media, and pop culture at large are manipulating them by hypersexualizing everything they can think of and practicing that age-old concept: Sex sells. These truths can empower our kids to make better choices about what they consume.

TALKING TO YOUR KIDS ABOUT SOFT PORN

We waited until our kids were eleven or twelve to talk about soft porn. By then they had already learned the basics about pornography, so it wasn't a big jump to introduce soft porn. I like to begin this conversation a year or two after puberty starts, but you know best when your child is developmentally ready.

AGES 11+

Key concept

Soft porn is different from pornography because the people are not entirely naked. They might have just a little bit of clothing on. They are also posing or acting in a way that is very sexual, because the purpose of soft porn is similar to that of pornography. It wants to catch your attention and keep your attention.

Instead of honoring and respecting the human

body, soft porn objectifies people to convince you to buy a product, watch a movie, read a book, or play a video game.

Activity

The point of this conversation and this exercise isn't just to show that soft porn exists but also how pop culture uses it to manipulate people and how we can evade their tricks.

Where are places we could encounter soft porn? Examples: video games, anime comic books, music videos, movies, magazines, television shows, romance novels, and social media.

What should we do when we encounter soft porn? Sample strategies:

- Always start by asking this question: "Is this honoring and respecting the whole person, or is it objectifying them?"
- If the answer is "objectifying," don't engage with that content.
- If sex is being used to catch your attention and keep you watching or sell you a product, move on.

Other tips for avoiding becoming desensitized to soft porn:

- Don't put soft porn in front of your eyes and dwell on it.

- If a pop-up ad or commercial comes up that features soft porn, turn it off.
- If you can't watch the show or listen to the music with your grandma or your little brother, maybe you shouldn't consume it on your own.
- If you notice soft porn on your social media or other apps and you are lingering to look at it, consider stepping away from your device.
- If you're unsure whether something you're consuming is soft porn and should be avoided, pray and ask God for his wisdom (James 1:5).

HAVE MORE THAN ONE CONVERSATION

Covering the topics of wise media consumption, objectification, and soft porn should not be a one-time conversation. These are topics that you should revisit often. Make it a practice to help your kids see the tricks the media is trying to play on them when you watch TV or movies and see commercials or advertisements. Be sure to call out objectification when it's happening. Don't let things slide because it might be uncomfortable to talk about. But even more, make an effort to model the opposite of objectification: Humans are made in the image of God and are therefore worthy of dignity, honor, and respect. Make that a topic of conversation even more often. Helping our kids see themselves and others in this light is one of the best ways to help them see pornography for the dangerous evil that it is.

Colossians 3:2–3 tells us, "Set your minds on things above, not on earthly things. For you died and your life is now hidden with Christ in God." This is exactly what I want for my kids as they grow up in a culture that trains them from a young age to be desensitized to sexualized images and content—and then to either dismiss it or crave it.

I don't want them to think sex is wrong or bad. Instead, I want them to recognize when sex is being used outside of God's original design and not settle for less than that. Let's step into these conversations with joy instead of dread. This is our chance to offer our kids the best!

IT'S TIME TO REFLECT

- Did you grow up in a family that talked about inappropriate, hypersexualized content, or was your family more likely to ignore it? When you encounter those things with your kids, is your first inclination to discuss it with them or pretend you don't see it? Explore the reason behind your answer and consider if you'd change anything.
- If you encountered an ad campaign like the Kraft Mac & Cheese one, how would you discuss it with your children?
- If you have never practiced media literacy with your children, what's the first step you can take this week?
- Are there ways you can reject soft porn in your own life as well as that of your kids? What's the first thing that comes to your mind?
- Are you willing to risk being seen as uptight, overly religious, or old-fashioned because of your views on porn and pop culture? If not, consider asking God to strengthen you to have a countercultural mindset.

PART TWO

How to Talk to Your Kids About Porn

SIX

Create a Healthy Sexual
Culture in Your Home

While this is a book about pornography, the conversation about sex matters too. If we only tell our kids that porn is bad but don't tell them the rest of the story—that sex is a gift from God, designed by him to be beautiful and good—then they are missing out on something incredibly important for their sexual health.

Helping our kids turn from the dangers of pornography is critically important, but so is helping them develop a healthy understanding of God's design for sex. We want them to see people as fully human, to cherish and uphold them, not objectify and dismiss them.

When parents ask me, "How do I talk to my kids about sex?" I tell them, "It's a hundred little conversations sprinkled in the middle of your everyday life." As we're talking with our kids about sex, remember that God's promise through Jesus is life to the full, which includes sex. I love the way Megan Michelson of Birds & Bees says it: "We've got a good story to tell!"[1] The subject of sex isn't something to shy away from; it's good news for a broken, hurting world.

Parents feel so intimidated by having "the talk" because they think it's a one-time conversation where they have to sit down with a script or a book and have a big, formal discussion. Or they take their preteen on a trip and spend a whole weekend talking about sex and the changing body. They've never broached the topic before, and now, seemingly out of the blue, they have to cover it all. No wonder these parents feel stressed!

I'm not saying don't use books or take your child on a trip to celebrate growing up. But I encourage you to also look for the organic and teachable moments in your everyday life and use them to talk to your kids about these things. You'll find the topic of sex becomes a lot less scary and a lot more comfortable. I want that for my kids. And I bet you want it for yours. Like the quote attributed to Dr. Howard Hendricks says, "We shouldn't be afraid to discuss what God wasn't afraid to create."

I find these teachable moments happen often. For example, I was standing in the kitchen with my then ten-year-old and he was making his lunch when he asked, "Are pheromones and hormones the same thing?"

"No, they're not," I said. "But let me tell you how they're different and what they do!"

I knew he'd been learning about ants and pheromones, and that was the source of his question. I also knew he was familiar with the idea of hormones because they were a frequent topic of conversation between my midlife hormones and all the teens and preteens in our home. So I took advantage of a teachable moment and jumped in.

I told him that God created some ants to be able to release

chemicals into the air called pheromones that other ants can sense and react to. Pheromones are one way insects and animals communicate. They're amazing!

> ## TALKING TO YOUR KIDS ABOUT HORMONES
>
> ### AGES 7+
>
> **Key concept**
>
> Hormones help our body change from a child to a grownup. They do things like make a girl's breasts grow and a boy's voice change. They help hair grow on men's faces and on men and women's private parts and under their arms.
>
> Sometimes hormones can make us feel grumpy, sad, or irritated. And they also help our bodies be able to make babies! Hormones are very important and a really wonderful part of God's design.

That was the whole conversation. There was no shame, no embarrassment, and no fear. We just had an easy conversation about puberty, with a nod to sex and reproduction, right in the middle of our kitchen at lunch time. That talk lasted less than ten minutes. It was one of many we'd already had and would have in the years to come.

This is one example of what it looks like to create a healthy sexual culture in your home: a fun little puberty talk with a ten-year-old. And yes, it was fun! Even though he did grimace a little when I mentioned that part of puberty was growing hair on our private parts. The thing is, both of us felt comfortable having this conversation because our family has worked hard from the time our kids were little to create a healthy and safe sexual culture in our home.

We never kept puberty talks hidden from the kids. As each child went through it, we were *all* going through it, so we *all* talked about it. Not in a way that pointed a finger at the hormone-crazed adolescent, but so other family members could offer support and understanding for a sibling that was going through a sometimes-challenging transition. There was no need for embarrassment or fear about the process of growing up.

We discussed the human body and our bodies with a sense of wonder and awe at what God created. There was understanding and compassion for one another when raging hormones (theirs or mine) made things tough. There were honest, age-appropriate answers given when they asked questions, and we moved forward with those conversations at their pace as much as possible. It was sometimes awkward, often funny, and now that we're in the teen and young adult years, I'll say it has been fully worth it.

MY SEX EDUCATION

Growing up, I was blessed with a beautiful and innocent childhood. I lived in a sweet, safe bubble; like many families in the eighties and nineties, mine hardly talked about sex. Around the age of nine or ten, I remember my parents telling my younger brother and me where babies came from. I don't remember them using the word "sex." It was more about reproduction. They did explain the mechanics of how the baby was created, and I vividly recall that part being awkward and my brother and me covering our ears. We still laugh about that memory.

I don't remember my family talking about sex or reproduction again—or puberty at all—until I was about thirteen. My mom gave me the book nearly every Christian teen read back then: *Preparing for Adolescence*. I think that was a good move on my mom's part. She was using one of the few tools available to her at the time to broach these topics with me.

The only trouble was, we didn't talk about the book when I finished. I don't know if I clammed up like a typical teenager or if my mom just didn't know how to talk to me about it. Maybe it was a combination of both. I definitely had questions. But because we didn't have a culture in our home where we talked about these things, I didn't ask. Through my high school years I realized that having sex was a choice, and God's design was to save sex for marriage. That was about the extent of my sex education.

Some kids in my position would have learned about sex from their friends. But I was homeschooled and raised in the church. It wasn't common to have open discussions about sex in either of those settings. Most of my friends were in the same circumstances. They knew as little as I did—they weren't going to be any help. Not that I was asking for info. I wasn't! Because, the truth was, since we didn't talk about sex at home, I was not comfortable bringing it up. It would have been so embarrassing. I knew sex had been created by God and that it wasn't bad, but there was a part of me that somehow still felt it might be.

I didn't have the maturity to understand it at the time, but the closedness of the topic made it feel bad. It was just so confusing and uncomfortable. Even if I did have questions, I didn't want to ask them. I don't blame my parents for their approach to this topic. They did the best they could with what they knew and with what was available to them. And they did an amazing job at keeping me safe from a lot of the ugliness in the world. They just didn't have a lot of resources for cultivating a healthy sexual culture in our family.

As I have grown in my own understanding of healthy sexuality, I've realized that not making the topic of sex an open conversation in our family contributed to some of the sexual struggles I faced later in my life. Not surprisingly, those struggles became a part of my marriage. Because I came into marriage feeling embarrassed about sex at best, and ashamed at worst, it took Aaron and me years to learn to talk about sex honestly and comfortably with each other. I'm glad for the work we've done and the growth that has come, but there was struggle and even heartache along the way. We didn't know how to talk about sex or our sexual relationship in a healthy way. He came from the same background I did, so we really didn't know what we were doing when it came to having conversations about sexual things. We both had expectations, struggles, questions, and disappointments when it came to our sex life. But we also didn't know how to share those with each other or with anyone else. It had been a "we don't talk about that" topic for so much of our lives that it was hard to make the switch into a new way of thinking and doing.

In addition, it felt embarrassing to admit that our newly-wed sex life wasn't "all sex, all the time." We were still figuring it all out, but every TV show and movie, and popular culture as a whole, implied everyone else was constantly having amazing sex. Even in the Christian culture we were a part of, there was this weird juxtaposition of not talking about sex before marriage and then the moment we were married there was an expectation, and plenty of jokes, that sex would be incredible and happen often without any issues or problems.

There were books on married sex, but many of them made sex seem all about the husband's pleasure and didn't address the wife's at all. And they didn't teach us how to talk about sex openly and unashamedly. They felt more like, "Try these new positions, be sexy, and everything will be fine!" None of this seemed right, but I didn't know what to do. Looking back, I have such a tenderness for that girl I once was. I wish so much I could help her navigate those early years of marriage and create a healthy sex life much sooner.

A DIFFERENT SEXUAL EDUCATION

Recognizing where Aaron and I weren't equipped to navigate our own sexual health helped us decide to do things a little differently when we had our own kids. Like all parents, we wanted to give our kids the best. That included a healthy view of sex that would one day help them have a happy and healthy sex life in marriage. We had experienced the struggle and then the health that came after healing. We wanted to equip our kids with the tools to navigate any struggle they might encounter far sooner, and with far less heartache.

Consider it this way: As parents, we worry about giving our kids the best food, the best toys, the best books, the best opportunities, the best classes and lessons, and the best education. Yet we often overlook giving them the best in terms of a healthy sexual outlook and future. We are missing an important part of their physical, emotional, and spiritual health. Our sexuality is a *big* part of our whole selves, and when we ignore it, pretend it isn't there, or are afraid to talk to our kids about it, we are doing them a great disservice.

That is why our family decided to walk a new path. We wanted our kids to come to adulthood and marriage better equipped than we were, with the understanding that sex isn't shameful, scary, or bad. In fact, we wanted them to know that sex is sacred, beautiful, and a gift! There are a few ways that we can easily start to do this.

1. Use anatomically correct language.

One of the best ways to clearly communicate that sex is not shameful is through the language we use. Parents sometimes act embarrassed or ashamed of the sexual parts of our bodies. But our kids need to know that every part of them is beautifully designed by God. Using the actual name for every part of the body can be an effective way to do this.

It banishes any shame related to the sexual organs. After all, kids see their entire body as an amazing machine. They're fascinated by how it works, and they want to understand it. They want to know why their body is different from yours and from their brother's or sister's. They aren't afraid, embarrassed, or ashamed of it. But when we parents start calling a penis a wee-wee and a vagina a pee-pee, or whatever your family says, then we are inadvertently attaching shame to those organs. We don't make up fake names for their elbows or eyebrows. So why would we make up a name for breasts or a penis? We don't have to! And we shouldn't. Using anatomically correct language is one of the easiest ways to begin creating a healthy sexual culture in your home.

It provides a layer of protection. God forbid your child would ever be molested in any way, but if they were, being able to accurately say where they were touched goes a long way in getting them help and making their story believable. The same is true if someone were to show them pornography. It is a powerful testimony for the child to be able to say, "That person showed me pornography. It was pictures of . . ." and to state what body part they saw. It's terrible to imagine that someone would argue that your child's story was not credible because they said "wee-wee" instead of the actual name of a sexual organ, but it could happen. So knowing and using the accurate names adds another layer of protection for your child.

Anatomically correct language should be used with respect. Many parents I talk to are on board with these ideas, but they wonder, "How do I keep my kid from using those words in public and totally embarrassing me or making other people uncomfortable?"

I share about one time when we were at the zoo, and we saw an elephant peeing. One of my kids was about five and yelled loudly and with absolute delight, "Hey, look! That elephant is peeing, and his penis is *gigantic!*" Every single person around us laughed. And I bet everyone was thinking the same thing because the elephant's penis *was* gigantic. My child wasn't being rude or crass or even inappropriate. However, I was aware there may have been people that were bothered, offended, or embarrassed in that moment.

That's why a little bit later I reminded that child of a conversation we'd had in our family many times: "These words need to be used with respect. Next time you have a thought like that, and you want to share it, you can just come tell me, okay?"

It is entirely appropriate to give our kids limits. This explanation makes sense to kids and doesn't attach shame. It's also a way to show respect for other people who have a different way of doing things.

TALKING TO YOUR KIDS ABOUT BODY PARTS

YOUNGER KIDS

Simply start talking this way with your kids from the beginning. They will grow up never knowing anything different and be really comfortable with all the words. There are so many opportunities all day long to practice using accurate names for every body part.

Practice accurate names of body parts during bath time, dressing/undressing, using the bathroom, or—if there's also a baby in the house—when nursing or changing a diaper. We can use those moments to refer to all body parts by their real names without shame or awkwardness. That said, if a child possesses absolutely no inhibitions about shouting about body parts in public places, you can communicate something like this:

Remember that the words we use for our private parts are not bad words, because our bodies have no bad parts. But these words need to be used with respect. They're private words for private parts, so we don't shout them out for everyone to hear. Next time you have a thought like that, and you want to share it, you can just come tell me, okay?

OLDER KIDS

If you've never used the real names for sexual body parts, have a conversation with your older child and let them know you're "changing" the names of things. Your conversation could go something like this:

> Now that you're older, it's important that we use the real, scientific names for our private parts. The names a doctor would use. You may know them already. They aren't bad words because there are no bad parts of your body.

> Keeping things matter-of-fact helps ease the awkwardness—not that there won't be some as you make the transition. It's okay if it's awkward. Just don't let that stop you from giving your kids the language they need to create a healthy view of sex now and in the future.

2. Embrace curiosity.

Another thing you can do to keep sex from feeling shameful is remembering that your child's curiosity about their body, your body, where babies come from, and even sex is not bad. It's usually totally normal! Most of the time we don't have to freak out when our kids are curious about sex or their bodies. In fact, it's important that we remain calm. When our kid asks us a question that makes our heart rate speed up, our facial expression should stay the same, our voice shouldn't get high and squeaky, and we definitely shouldn't shut them down by responding, "We don't talk about those things!"

Embracing our kid's curiosity doesn't mean we tell them everything related to sex and the human body any time they ask a question. We answer calmly and honestly, giving only as much information as they need at that time.

When I was pregnant with our third baby, our oldest was only three and a half years old, but he was well aware there was a baby growing inside my tummy. And he was thinking about it—we just didn't realize it until one night at the dinner table when he asked, "So how did that baby get in your tummy anyway?"

Aaron's eyes got wide and he kind of froze. He was the opposite of calm. I think it was because he imagined we were going to have to tell our three-year-old son all about sex right that minute.

Of course we didn't. Instead I said something along the lines of, "God designed mommies with eggs inside of them, and he designed daddies with sperm inside of them. Sperm kind of look like little fish, and when the sperm and the egg meet, they make a baby!"

Our son looked at me for a moment, said "Okay," and went back to eating dinner. That was all he needed to know at that moment. Kids don't need the hose turned on full blast. They just need bits of information sprinkled on them.

Unless it's something they need to know for safety reasons,

we can also let our older kids lead the way with how much info they're ready for. When one of our kids was a preteen, they once asked me, "How do people not have a whole bunch of kids once they get married if having sex gets the woman pregnant?" I love when our kids ask these kinds of questions, because it proves that they can ask us anything and we will answer calmly and honestly.

I started by summarizing the information they already knew: (1) People don't have to be married to make a baby. (2) A woman can get pregnant only a few days of the month, so having sex doesn't always mean a baby is made. Then I waited to see if there were more questions. There were.

"How do you know which days you cannot get pregnant?" they asked.

I reminded them about ovulation, which we had learned about during puberty talks. "But there are other ways to avoid getting pregnant. Obviously not having sex is the most effective option. But when you're married you want to have sex with your spouse. So a couple will often use something called birth control, which helps them not get pregnant. I can explain more about birth control if you want, but some of the info can be a little . . . personal. Since you're far from marriage you don't have to know all those details until you're a little older, but if you want to know right now, I'm happy to discuss it with you."

This child thought about this for a little while and said, "I think I'll wait." And when that child needs that information, I'll revisit it and share it all calmly and honestly.

Embracing our kid's curiosity—instead of shutting it down or ignoring it—has led to honest and shame-free conversations. Developing comfort around these topics isn't important just for them as kids and teens; it's going to prove invaluable when they enter marriage and have the skills to talk about their sexual relationship freely and honestly.

One important note: If your child is curious about their own body or yours, there is usually nothing to worry about. However, if they act out something sexual with another child or another child acts out something sexual with them, you need to pause and ask some questions.

Many of us probably played "house" when we were growing up and maybe acted out having a baby or breastfeeding it. Those games are generally innocent and harmless. However, acting out anything sexual and especially touching body parts is different. Given the growing number of children being exposed to pornography, even at a young age like six or eight, there are a growing number of child-upon-child sexual abuse cases. It's not anything any of us ever want to imagine, but we have to be aware of it. We must ask uncomfortable questions and get help for our kids or other kids if needed.

TALKING TO YOUR KIDS ABOUT REPRODUCTION

YOUNGER KIDS

Key concept

God designed mommies with eggs inside of them, and he designed daddies with sperm inside of them. Sperm look kind of like little fish. When the sperm and the egg meet, they make a baby!

OLDER KIDS

Sample dialogue

Child: If a woman gets pregnant by having sex, how do people not have lots of kids once they get married?

Parent: First, people don't have to be married to make a baby. Also, a woman cannot get pregnant all the time—it's only possible a few days of each month. So having sex doesn't always mean a baby is made.

Child: How do you know which days you cannot get pregnant?

Parent: A woman can only get pregnant if she is ovulating. Ovulation is when her body releases an egg into her fallopian tube. If the egg gets fertilized by sperm, a pregnancy can begin. There are also ways to avoid getting pregnant. Obviously not having sex is the most effective option. But when you're married you want to have sex with your spouse. So a couple will often use something called birth control, which helps them not get pregnant. I can explain more about birth control if you want, but some of the info can be a little personal. Since you're far from marriage you don't have to know all those details until you're a little older, but if you want to know right now, I'm happy to discuss it with you.

3. Cultivate an attitude of honor and respect toward the body.

For the most part, kids already see that their bodies are an amazing creation. They're fascinated by things like burping and farting and sneezing and boogers and bad breath because they are funny and interesting. As parents, we need to engage with them in their wonder. Teach your child how their body works. Get out the human-body books and learn why elbows and knees bend, how their brain makes enough electricity to power a light-bulb, and that their tongue has eight thousand tastebuds. As they grow older we should constantly remind them that their body, the human body, is the most incredibly designed machine in the universe. This goes such a long way in creating an attitude of body positivity and respect.

Cultivating this attitude of respect and honor is an important tool in protecting our kids from pornography. When they are taught that their body is designed in God's image, they will realize that it is worthy of respect and honor.

If kids are raised in an environment that sees the human body as fearfully and wonderfully made, as worthy of celebration and respect, they'll be more likely to see and call out the lie of pornography, which neither celebrates nor respects the body and the soul.

I know it can feel scary to talk to your kids about sex. But the healthy sexual culture you are creating that allows for these conversations to take place isn't just protecting them from potential danger. These talks are the foundation that allows you to have all those other conversations about things like pornography, sexting, and sextortion. I can tell you from experience that those conversations will be easier when you've created a culture of safety and trust around sexual topics.

Remember, this is an investment in your child's future and in helping them become people with sexual integrity. This means more than not sleeping around or not watching porn. It's treating their fellow humans with dignity, respect, and honor. It's seeing themselves and others as people made in the image of God. What a gift to your children!

IT'S TIME TO REFLECT

- Did you grow up in a home where it was comfortable and you were encouraged to ask questions about sexual matters, puberty, or the human body? How did that impact your childhood, adolescence, and even your marriage?
- Describe what you'd like the sexual culture to look like in your family now. If there are things that don't match your goal, what changes can you identify that you can begin to make now?
- What stories from this chapter resonated with you the most? If any of them made you uncomfortable, reflect on why and consider what you'd change with your own kids.
- Pick one of the three action steps from this chapter— using anatomically correct language, embracing curiosity, and creating an attitude of respect and honor. How can you begin applying that action right now?

SEVEN

Give Your Kids a Porn Plan

Every time I tell parents they need to give their kids a porn plan, they chuckle. It's an awkward title, I know. But parents don't forget it. Change the name if you want, but no matter what, your child needs a plan to safely respond to pornography. Opening up the conversation and giving them a plan for what to do when they see it (and an escape plan if they're using it) is the most important thing you can do to help your kids fight pornography! A porn plan is more important than filters, parental controls on their devices, monitoring their texts, or limiting their screen time. The most important thing you can do to help your kids fight pornography is to simply *talk to them about it* and *keep talking.*

WHEN TO BEGIN?

When parents ask me what age their kid should be when they start talking to them about pornography, I tell them to have the first conversation by the time their kid is five or six. Many parents push back at this. "But surely that's too young," they argue.

I understand—in a sane world, that *is* too young. But that's not the world we're living in.

Consider these scenarios:

- A five-year-old sits in the shopping cart with his mom's phone and watches videos on YouTube while she grocery shops.
- A six-year-old wants to draw and searches online for "kitty cat" to find pictures to copy.
- A seven-year-old plays games on a tablet in his bedroom while he has his rest time.
- An eight-year-old completes school assignments on his school-issued Chromebook.
- A nine-year-old plays video games at a friend's house.
- A ten-year-old gets her first smartphone for her birthday.

Any of these normal and harmless scenarios could result in accidental pornography exposure.

- The five-year-old sees new show suggestions appear on the screen after his ends. He taps one.
- The six-year-old scrolls through the images of the "kitty cat" she googled.
- The seven-year-old taps a pop-up ad that appears on the screen while he plays his game.
- The eight-year-old opens a message a classmate sent to everyone on their Chromebook before school started.
- The nine-year-old's friend chats with a stranger while they play their online video game.

- The ten-year-old plays with her new phone that comes with no preinstalled safety controls.

The hope is that by talking to your kids about pornography at a young age, you can help them be prepared *before* they see it. Instead of doing damage control after exposure, when the child may be paralyzed with shock, fear, and shame—or maybe even a little curious to see more—you've empowered them to respond quickly and safely to whatever images appear before their eyes. As much as possible we want to get ahead of our kids on this.

After I convince parents that they need to talk to their kids ages five and up about pornography, the next argument comes up. "But my kids don't even know about sex yet." To which I always reply, "That's fine. At such a young age there is no reason for them to know pornography and sex are connected."

Here is what I mean: Your young kids don't have to know about sex for them to understand that pornography is dangerous. You give them just what they need to stay safe right now. The information about sex and pornography will come a little later when they are developmentally ready, when they begin to ask questions, or as things come up in their experiences. But when they are young, you give just what they need to know to stay safe now.

Another way to think about it is this: We don't go into graphic detail about what could happen if our kids cross the street without us and get hit by a car. We simply say, "You could get hurt, so don't cross the street alone." In the same way, we don't need to go into graphic detail about all the elements of pornography and its harmful effects. We just say, "It's my job to keep you safe from this thing that is bad for you."

TALKING TO YOUR KIDS ABOUT PORNOGRAPHY

AGES 5 TO 10

For the youngest kids, a porn plan is

1. a very simple definition of pornography and
2. what to do if they see it.

Key concept

Pornography is pictures or movies of people with no clothes on who are showing their private parts.

Sample dialogue

Hey sweetie, I need to tell you about something called pornography. Pornography is pictures or movies of people with no clothes on and showing their privates. We don't show our private parts to other people, and we don't look at other people's private parts, so pornography is not something we should be looking at.

If you ever see those kinds of pictures or movies on a computer, a tablet, or a phone, or if someone tries to show them to you, here's what you need to do:

You simply look away, shut the computer, turn over the phone, or turn off the tablet. If someone is trying to show it to you, use your strongest voice and say, "I don't want to look at that." And then you just walk away. Walk away from the screen you were on or walk away from the person.

Then find Mom or Dad or another safe grown-up and tell them what you saw. You won't be in trouble for seeing pornography. We want you to tell us what happened because talking about it is one of the ways we keep you safe.

That's all you have to say! See how easy it is? There is no need to mention sex or give the kids details. They need just enough information to keep them safe. Over the years, as they are developmentally ready, you keep giving them more information as it's needed, a little bit at a time.

You might feel concern about your kids learning the word "pornography." But most young kids don't have any of the negative associations with porn that adults have. They don't know the content, the shame, or the things it is associated with. To them it is just another word, like "fingernails," "butterflies," or "book." We are the ones who carry the heavy weight associated with the word "pornography."

Another reason it's important to use this real language is for the child's protection. If anyone ever showed your child pornography, it is important for them to be able to correctly identify it by both the definition and the title. This gives their story validity. It's painful to imagine a day when that would be necessary, but if it were to arise, I'd rather have my child prepared. In the same way you'd prepare for what to do if they get lost in an amusement park, you must prepare your child for what to do if they encounter pornography.

It's a good idea to practice the porn plan together. Act out your child's response to seeing porn on various devices and then when someone shows it to them. Brainstorm a list of safe adults to talk to if Mom or Dad isn't around. Reiterate that they won't be in trouble for telling the truth about what they saw. You want to talk about it and get help! Practice the plan more than once the first time around and then keep practicing once in a while. A good way to help your kids remember how to respond is to share the three *T*s:

Turn it off.
Tell a parent.
Talk about it.

By preparing your kids from a young age, you are arming them with weapons for the fight! You are giving them a better chance at saying no to porn.

HOW TO CONTINUE?

As your kids grow older, the porn plan needs to grow with them. You aren't done talking just because you had conversations when they were little. You are never done talking! Silence is the best way for things to stay hidden and for hurt to fester. Preteens and teens might respond to you with silence, but they are still listening to you. By not being silent you're showing them that you are a safe place to bring those hurts.

If you've shared a porn plan with them when they were little, you'll be adding to the conversation with the new things kids could encounter as they enter the preteen and teen years. But first I want to address the parent that is starting at the preteen or teen age. You might feel like it is too late for you to talk to your kids about pornography and especially to give them a porn plan. You might think, *I'm sure they know what porn is, and they might have even seen it. They don't need a definition. And it would just be too embarrassing for both of us to bring this up now. They're too old.* Isn't it funny how our discomfort with the topic of pornography causes us to make the same excuses to get out of the conversation no matter the age of our kids? You know the answer: Whether they're young or old, we have to talk to our kids.

It's critical for you to talk to your preteen or teen about pornography even if you think they've heard about it from someone else or have seen it. They need to know your thoughts and beliefs, not just what Google, their friends, teachers, or popular culture thinks about pornography.

I guarantee your child will not be jumping up and down for joy. They may get silent or uncomfortable, say no, ask you to stop, or try to leave. Encourage them to stay and listen. If they are really closed to the conversation, explain that it's too important to avoid talking about, but you'll give them time to get ready. Suggest talking about it in a few days or in a week. When you do talk, give them a definition of what pornography is. Even if they have heard of it before, give them *your* definition.

The last thing you need to cover in the conversation is what to do if they see pornography. It's time to give them their porn plan!

TALKING TO YOUR KIDS ABOUT PORNOGRAPHY

AGES 10+

Sample dialogue

So there's something we need to talk about. It's called "pornography." You may have heard of it before or maybe even seen it. But I want you to know it's bad for your body, brain, and heart. In fact, pornography is dangerous, so we need to talk about it.

Pornography is pictures or videos of people wearing no clothes and exposing all parts of their bodies and engaging in sexual acts with one another for the purpose of causing sexual excitement for the viewer.

You can accidentally find pornography in many ways:

- an innocent search for something online,
- a pop-up ad,
- a friend or a random kid on their baseball team showing you,
- on video game chats,
- in comic books, and
- so many more places.

There are two reasons I am sharing this with you:

1. Porn is everywhere and easily accessible; you need to be on your guard.
2. You didn't do anything wrong if you find porn. Most first-time exposure is purely accidental.

If you find pornography, turn the device off, turn the phone over, close the laptop. If someone has shown it to you, tell them you don't want to look at that and then remove yourself from the conversation. If you're at school or at a game or practice, walk away. If you are at their house or hanging out with them, call me and I'll come get you. The important thing is to get away from pornography or from the person who showed it to you.

Based on personal experience, it's pretty common for teens to not have much to say after you give them a porn plan. My kids are exceptionally comfortable with the topic of pornography, but they still were not very interested in talking to me about it after I gave them these scenarios. Your teen will probably be the same. That's okay. They heard what they need to do if they see pornography, and that's the most important part.

Make sure they understand the last part of the porn plan and know that they need to come talk to you after they see porn. This is critical! There are a few ways you can do this:

1. Be sure they know that you are on their side.
2. Establish a special phrase or code word they can use so you will know to pick them up right away if a friend shows them something inappropriate.
3. Assure them that if they saw porn, you will not be mad or blame them. You want to help them heal from what they've seen.

This conversation will probably feel awkward, embarrassing, and challenging. You can tell your child that you know that the conversation after they've seen porn might feel even harder, but your love for them is big enough to handle it.

INVITING OTHERS INTO HARD CONVERSATIONS

A valuable addition to this conversation is giving your kids a few people they can talk to if they've seen porn or are using porn and don't feel comfortable talking to you. Be brave enough to invite others into the conversation with you. The most important thing isn't being your child's number one confidant. As parents we want that. But if that desire keeps your child from sharing important pieces of information, you need to let that go.

Here are simple steps for inviting others into this conversation:

1. Before talking to your child, think of three or four people you'd like them to talk to about these issues.
2. Share the names with your child and ask them to come up with their own list. Hopefully there's a few names from the two lists that overlap. If not, keep trying until you have a few people both of you feel comfortable including.

3. Let those people know they're on your child's list and ask if they feel comfortable having discussions on these topics with your child. Let everyone know that they are expected to share with you what they talk about. These people are your partners, not a wall for your child to hide behind.

4. Give your child the contact information for the people on their list so they can talk to them without asking you ahead of time.

Pornography has so much fear and shame attached to it that we seldom think of working as a team and fighting it together. We might be comfortable talking about it within our family unit, but inviting others in feels incredibly vulnerable and scary. Nevertheless, doing so is a powerful way to let your child know that you love them so much and so value their safety that you're willing to do whatever it takes to protect them—even letting someone else talk to them first. Even letting other people in to see your mess.

As a parent, it's also powerful for us to know that we have support on our side. I'm honored to serve in this friend role for others. How incredible to have a safe place to share our problems and have people who listen, pray, hold us accountable, and hold us up! This is one more way we can break the silence around pornography and start healing.

WHATEVER IT TAKES

Remember, as parents we are called to walk with our kids through the most challenging stuff to keep them safe and help them grow up healthy! You don't get a pass on this because they are too young, too old, already know about porn, or won't open up to you. Do whatever it takes to talk to your kids about pornography, and then to keep talking about it.

Think about it this way: You don't opt out of fire or emergency drills because you worry your kid will be afraid of an emergency happening. That's ridiculous! You know that preparing will keep them safer.

You also don't stay silent about inappropriate touch because you don't want to take away your kids' innocence. Giving them the tools to protect themselves will help safeguard so much more of their innocence than if you say nothing. Instead of looking at these conversations and strategies with dread, let's consider that they are a gift to our children—both now and in the years to come. How wonderful to be building a culture of safety and trust with them!

IT'S TIME TO REFLECT

- Did anyone give you tools for responding to pornography exposure as a child or teen? If they had, would it have made a difference in your life?

- Using what you've learned from this chapter, craft a porn plan for your family. If you have children in different stages, make a plan for each child's specific needs.

- Who can you enlist to be on your parenting team? Text, email, or call them today and invite them to journey with you and your children.

- What is the number one thing you can do to help protect your kids from pornography? How will you offer that to your child today?

EIGHT

Respond with Compassion
Instead of Judgment

Of all the topics I cover in this book, this one holds a special place in my heart. God has used pornography to change the posture of my heart to one of compassion. For most of my life I would never have paired "compassion" with "pornography." I'd have used words like "disgust," "fear," "anger," "judgment," "shame," and "pride."

In the past I felt disgust for anyone who used pornography. I was afraid of it and anything and everything to do with it. Pornography made me angry, and the thought of anyone I knew or loved using it made me angry too. I held nothing but harsh judgment and disdain for anyone who used it. If they felt shame because they used pornography, in my mind that was totally deserved. And I felt pride that I'd never been tempted to use pornography, that it hadn't been a struggle for me.

I am not proud of any of those attitudes. I had a lot of spiritual pride that left no room for grace or compassion to anyone struggling with sexual sin. While I never would have chosen the avenue God used to show me the depth of my own sinful heart, I'm grateful that he gave me the opportunity to change. The compassion that grew in me wasn't just for users of pornography. God changed my heart to become more gracious and compassionate toward my children, my husband, family, friends, and even strangers.

HOW TO HAVE COMPASSIONATE CONVERSATIONS

Compassion is deeply important when your child comes to you and says, "I think I've seen porn." You need to wrap them in your arms and say, "I'm so sorry. Your heart must be hurting from seeing that." Your reaction in that moment needs to be one of compassion, not shame, anger, or judgment. This is your opportunity to be tender and loving when they need it the most.

When they've accidentally seen something

This happened with one of our children when they were eleven years old. It was Super Bowl Sunday, and though I didn't watch the game, I caught a few minutes of the half-time show. I couldn't believe what I was seeing—pole dancing and costumes that barely covered anything. It was soft porn. I was so glad we'd opted out of the Super Bowl again. But one of our children hadn't.

Our eleven-year-old had spent the afternoon at a friend's house where everyone was watching the Super Bowl. When the half-time show came on, no one turned it off, even when it got inappropriate.

When I realized our child had seen the show, I was bummed I hadn't thought to say, "Hey, when the half-time show comes on, you and your friend should go do something else. It's not going to be anything you need to watch." But I didn't even think about it. The truth is, we can't put a force field around our kids that provides absolute protection from all harm. We just do our best and pray for the rest.

It turned out that my best hadn't entirely shielded this child, but they remembered the tools we'd talked about and put them to use in that tricky situation. While getting ready for bed that night, I asked my child for thoughts about the show.

"It was weird and uncomfortable, Mom. I went into the bathroom for a while, and then I went in the kitchen and hung out by the food. And when I was in the room with the TV, I looked away as much as I could."

While I was sad that my kid had felt so uncomfortable, I was incredibly proud of the way it was handled. "I'm not disappointed with you," I assured them. "In fact, I'm so proud of your quick and creative thinking in an uncomfortable situation. You are not in trouble. You aren't responsible for other people making the wrong decision."

When I said I wasn't disappointed, their little body immediately relaxed, gratefully folding into my arms. I'm so glad to be a safe place for my kids to land in this difficult world.

Our child chose to be honest and tell us about watching the half-time show. It would have been easy to lie, thus avoiding my potential disappointment and the numerous conversations that would probably follow. I was grateful for their honesty because it opened the door for those important conversations. That was all we said on the subject that night. I didn't want to belabor it or overwhelm my kid. There was more to cover, but I planned to discuss it later with all the kids.

The next morning all five of us sat around the table for our morning devotions, and I brought the conversation back up. "So we need to talk a little bit more about the half-time show last night."

Some of the other kids protested. "But we didn't even see it!"

"Whether you saw it or not, there are things we need to discuss. You know who you're dealing with, right? The talk-about-everything mom."

They groaned and laughed but settled in.

"Your sibling did the best they could and had good ideas for how to handle it. But I want you to have more options for what to do in a similar situation. And I want you to put yourselves there so that if something like this happens to any of you, you'll know what to do." Together, we brainstormed ideas:

- Leave the room and go to the bathroom.
- Go the kitchen and hang out by the food.
- Tell your friend you want to do something else.
- Find a book to read.
- Draw.
- Suggest to other kids to go outside and play.
- See if anyone wants to play a game.
- Tell your friend's mom that you don't feel good and want to call your parents.
- Ask to go home.

The last two on the list were critical. I want our kids to know they don't have to stay anywhere or watch anything that makes them uncomfortable, even if everyone else—including the grown-ups—is watching and seems okay with it. Listening to the check in their own spirit, the voice telling them, "This doesn't feel right," is the most important thing. I will always support them in following their instincts.

As much as I wished our child hadn't seen that half-time show, I knew all the kids were better equipped for next time. Because I responded with compassion and grace instead of frustration or anger, it opened the doors of communication and allowed us all to have important conversations.

When they've intentionally consumed porn

But what about when your child comes to you and says, "I've been watching porn"? This one feels a little harder to face. It is normal to feel anger, sadness, fear, shame, judgment, and a whole host of unpleasant emotions upon a confession like that. And it may possibly feel even worse if your child doesn't confess and you stumble upon the truth yourself. Can you feel compassion in that moment? You can and you should.

In the same way that you'd wrap your arms around your child who was accidentally exposed to pornography and offer them comfort and words of care and love, you can do that for this child too. Imagine the hope you'd give that child if you said the following.

TALKING TO YOUR KIDS WHEN THEY'VE CONSUMED PORNOGRAPHY

ALL AGES

Key concept

I'm so sorry you've seen this. I know you must be hurting and confused right now. You might feel sad or scared too. I want you to know that what you've seen is

---

not God's plan for sex. It is what the devil has created to deceive and destroy people. But there is help and there is hope. And I want to help you find the way out.

I think this quote from Dr. Juli Slattery says it so well: "People are looking for help for their addictions and hope for their broken hearts. They want living water. If we run away or become judgmental or uncomfortable any time we see sexual pain, we will miss the greatest opportunities to enter the pain of their sexual brokenness and share the love of Jesus Christ."[1]

We don't have to miss an opportunity to share the compassion of Jesus just because our kids disappointed us. I've also learned to use compassion when talking to my kids about those who consume pornography. Because if I am spewing judgment and condemnation, my child is far less likely to come to me when he's the one who has been consuming pornography.

You aren't telling your kids you approve of watching porn. Of course not! But you can explain to your child how dangerous porn is because it impacts the brain, and that we want people who are addicted to get help. We want them to see the truth and not believe the lie. This allows your kids to see the gravity of the situation without instilling fear of coming to you when they need to. Compassion will pull our kids toward us rather than push them away.

COMPASSION TRANSFORMS

Before finding out about my husband's pornography addiction, I'd never thought about the reasons why someone would turn to pornography. I just judged them hard. But with each new thing I learned, I felt a tenderness grow in my heart for my husband and the darkness he'd been trapped in. You know that did not come from my own power—it was the supernatural power of God allowing that tenderness and compassion to grow in my heart. I think often of that time and how, for the first time in my life, I had the opportunity to understand these challenging and convicting words by C. S. Lewis: "To be a Christian means to forgive the inexcusable because God has forgiven the inexcusable in you."[2]

I know now that God gave me the opportunity to look at Aaron with compassion and grace so that in the years to come I could look with compassion at other men and women, boys and girls, who are also struggling with pornography use and addiction.

Just a few weeks ago I talked to a room of young men about the damage pornography use and porn addiction could bring to their lives. As I stood in front of them—the lone woman in the room and much older with different life experiences—I thought, *Wow, this is awkward.*

I could see many of them felt the same. They were fidgeting, giggling, looking at anything but me or their fellow attendees. Statistically I knew most of them were using porn occasionally and some much more. But as I began speaking and looking each one in the eyes, the awkwardness faded and all I felt for them was love, care, and compassion.

"You deserve so much more than porn is offering you," I told them. "You deserve to experience real love, intimacy, connection, safety, and belonging. Porn doesn't care about you having those things because porn doesn't care about you. But I do." And it was true. Compassion has transformed my heart.

IT'S TIME TO REFLECT

- Does compassion come easily for you? If not, reflect on why that might be.

- Imagine your child coming to you and confessing to seeing porn. Now imagine how you want to respond. Pray that the Lord will give you the ability to respond with compassion.

- Repeat that same scenario and imagine your child was involved in regular porn use and you discovered it instead of the child confessing. Pray that the Lord will give you compassion in these situations as well.

- If there has been a situation when you didn't respond with compassion, ask the Lord to help you apologize to your child and seek to be a place of peace for them rather than a place of judgment or fear.

- Think of a time in your parenting when you've experienced failure. Can you give that situation to God and ask him to take the burden and shower you with compassion?

NINE

Walk a Different Path

When one of my sons was fifteen years old, he was earning his Cyber Chip badge for Scouts. He had to watch videos on using the internet safely, create an internet safety plan, and have a discussion with a parent about what he'd learned. He and I laughed as he watched the videos and worked through the questions. "Do I really have to do this?" he joked. "I mean, don't they know who my mom is?"

The final step was a meeting with his Scout leader where he demonstrated what he'd learned. When his leader asked him if he'd ever encountered cyber bullying, my son said, "The only cyber bully I know is my mom. She hardly lets me use the internet." His leader laughed and got the joke. But he also asked more questions because my son's answer wasn't the norm.

Our kids have certainly walked a different road. Our oldest got his first smartphone at age eighteen, and our second son got his at seventeen. One of them still doesn't have social media and doesn't have a desire for it. The other didn't get it until he was almost nineteen.

Our sixteen-year-old and thirteen-year-old don't have their own smartphones yet, and they won't until they're driving or there's another compelling reason to have one. We plan to wait on social media accounts until they are eighteen—or later if they so choose.

Parents often tell me that it's impossible for their kids to not have a smartphone or social media. I reply that it isn't impossible, but I fully understand it can be difficult. Choosing this lifestyle for your family requires a lot of grace, flexibility, and laughter.

I didn't mind the title my son gave me. In fact, I laughed really hard when he told me. It doesn't bother me when our kids make jokes about me or their forced 1980s lifestyle, because laughing helps us cope. Like when one of our sons wanted to download Spotify onto his phone. I gave him my standard answer of, "Let me look up reviews on the safety of that app."

He good-naturedly rolled his eyes and said, "I was expecting that."

After a few minutes of reading, I said, "Oh, this checks out perfect, bud! You can totally get Spotify Kids. It has great safety ratings."

"Are you kidding?" he said. "I'm seventeen years old! I'm not going to download Spotify Kids!" It's not easy to shock our kids with my responses to tech requests, but he was genuinely taken aback.

I grinned at him. "Yes, I am kidding. You don't have to get Spotify Kids."

He shook his head and smiled. "Well, with you, we never really know."

"You're right," I said. And then we both laughed.

Being different is not easy. It's not easy for our kids, and it's not easy for us. But we believe so strongly in why we've done tech differently that we're willing to walk this road right alongside them.

WHEN THEY WERE YOUNGER

When our kids were younger (twelve and under), it was easy to keep a tight lid on technology. Our tech strategies were different from most families' lifestyles. We didn't have a TV or cable, but we watched movies or shows on the laptop. We didn't have video games or gaming systems, but the kids could play a few specific games at certain friends' houses or on their grandma's iPad. The kids didn't have Kindles to listen to audiobooks, but they could listen together on my phone. They didn't have tablets for drawing on, but they had endless stacks of paper, their own sketchbooks, and tons of art supplies. They couldn't play games on my phone, but if they wanted to make a video or take pictures, I usually let them (even better was having a digital camera of their own). If they wanted to look up a picture of a Pokémon character on my laptop, they had to ask. At first, they sat next to me while searching, and when they were older they sat in the same room.

By the later preteen years if they wanted to text a friend or talk on the phone, they could use mine or the safe phone we owned for all of them to use. We didn't watch movies in the car, but we all listened to books together. We shared adventures through the books we listened to as a family, and it created connections between us. When friends came over, they didn't play video games and they spent very little time on a screen, but they did get to bake cookies, build Legos, make forts in the living room, and do big, messy art projects.

Our lifestyle was different, but our kids didn't rebel. And with the exception of occasionally wishing we had video games, they were happy and content. We didn't focus on how bad tech was and chose to use tech and screens to enhance our life and creativity. We looked for ways to use it to bring us closer together, not pull us apart.

Of course, there were factors that made all this easier.

We were thoughtful about technology.

We have never denied our kids all tech. We didn't want to make technology and screens so forbidden that they were all the kids wanted. Also, technology brings a lot of good and important things to our lives. Living a no-tech life is not realistic for our world, nor would we be preparing them to use tech responsibly in the future by denying them all tech as they grew up. Instead we introduced it slowly and thoughtfully. Even more importantly, we made a big effort to help our kids engage in real-life relationships, activities, and adventures so that the siren call of technology was a little less powerful.

We were part of a like-minded community.

It also helped that we were part of a friend group that practiced the same tech norms. I didn't have to ask my friends what their tech policy was when my kids went over to play, because I already knew. And if our kids were over on a Friday night, I knew they'd ask our permission before showing a movie, no matter what the rating was. It made things so much easier for all of us to be on the same page.

If your family or kids don't have this kind of community, I agree that it makes choosing a different way of doing tech much harder. But the good news is that more and more parents are opting out of the old norms of giving their kids smartphones at ten years old and social media at thirteen. The enormous success of the 1000 Hours Outside community and Jonathan Haidt's book *The Anxious Generation* show that parents want something different for their kids. They're seeking alternatives. And that means that it's easier than ever for parents to find families opting for a slower intro to technology for their kids.

If you're looking for that community yourself, here are suggestions on where you can find it or how you can create it:

- Join a Wait Until 8th campaign at your child's school, and if they don't have one yet, start one.
- Invite fellow preschool moms and kids on regular play-dates to the park, beach, nature center, or your backyard, where there's lots of time for play and no time for screens.
- Join a play- and experience-focused community like 1000 Hours Outside, where you'll be inspired and encouraged by other families' screen-free adventures.
- When your kids' friends come over, invite them to put phones in a basket on the kitchen counter and then provide all kinds of screen-free activities including lots of snacks, board and card games, musical instruments, a fire pit and s'mores supplies, basketball, pickleball, ping pong or Spikeball, and art-making supplies. Make your house the place where fun happens regularly.
- Join an online community of parents passionate about keeping kids safe online, like *The Table* from Protect Young Eyes.
- Become involved in your school and community and bring in speakers on this topic to give parents the inspiration

and practical help they need to create a different life for their kids.

- Pick a book from the Resource Guide in the back of this book, and invite a group of friends to read and discuss it. Who knows where those conversations could lead!

Even if you don't find a like-minded community, I believe that it's our job as parents to hold our ground and do what's best for our kids in the long run. This should be done with as much sympathy, understanding, grace, and support as possible. It isn't easy to be the kid without a smartphone or social media.

We also have to be flexible. In our family we have some hard-and-fast norms (we'll never agree that sexting can be safe), but with other things we've remained open to changing as the kids get older. We just made every effort to keep sight of our ultimate goal: to keep our kids as safe as possible, and as engaged in real life as possible, while learning to use tech responsibly.

We delayed giving our kids a phone.

This is when most parents say to me, "Yeah, yeah, all of this sounds really good, but when should I actually give my kids a phone?" We all want someone to just give us the answer to this question that has become one of the biggest and most challenging decisions in modern-day parenting. I'll give an answer, but it won't make you happy: Give your kids a phone when you're ready for them to see porn.

I told you that you weren't going to like it.

I know reading that sentence makes it easy to feel scared and overwhelmed or, if your kid already has a phone, defensive and upset. Take a deep breath and sit for a minute with that uncomfortable statement. Remember, my goal with this book is not to scare you but to provide support, education, and tools to empower you in the battle against porn. So keep breathing and let's talk about my statement.

It's not one that I came up with, although I agree with it fully. I heard it the first time as I was driving through the Wisconsin countryside late at night, headed to speak at a conference. I was listening to my friend Ginny Yurich's podcast, *1000 Hours Outside*. When the guest said it, I shouted "Amen!" and fist pumped in agreement. I'd never heard it put so bluntly and I appreciated that. But then I stopped to think and asked myself, "Knowing this is true, how should it impact my parenting?"

The real question we need to ask is not "When should I give my kid a phone?" but "Knowing how easy it is for my kids to be exposed to porn and a whole host of other troubling things on smartphones, how can I best prepare them to make wise and safe choices when they do get a phone?" Here are key answers to this question.

Delay giving your child a smartphone for as long as possible. Giving your kid the gift of a childhood not tethered to a screen is a rare and beautiful thing these days. Plus, it gives those little brains more time to develop before they're faced with all the negative things that will be at their fingertips the moment that smartphone is placed in their hands. Give them a safe phone to start with and let them use that for as long as possible.[1]

Give your kids a porn plan. Before you ever place a phone in their hands, go over the porn plan that we talked about in chapter 7 and remind them to talk to you immediately if they see porn.

When you do give your kids a smartphone, enable all the safety features you can. Use the parental controls on the phone, block the most troubling websites, use monitoring software, keep apps to the bare minimum, know their passwords, and do random phone checks. Remind your kids that you are their partner in tech and not their parole officer. You are there to help keep them safe, not catch them messing up.

Have many conversations with them about safe phone practices. Conversation is the number one tool in protecting our kids from pornography. Routers, software, and parental controls are important. But if our kids can't talk to us when those things fail, then all the safeguards we have put in place mean nothing. Talking with our kids doesn't mean they'll never see porn. But the negative impact can be greatly lessened if we've prepared them for how to respond and if they know they can talk to us about it.

The bottom line is that there is no magical right age for getting a smartphone. We decided early on that we'd make our kids wait until eighteen. That was easy when the kids were all under the age of seven and had no idea that they could even have their own phone. But as they got older and began driving or needed a phone for classes or work where everyone communicated on an app, or they needed to talk to people over text, or whatever the reason, we found that setting a specific age wasn't the best way forward. Instead of having a set-in-stone rule, we needed to create a cultural norm in our family that kids get a smartphone when it's truly necessary. And when that time comes, we'll have done our best to prepare them to use it safely and wisely.

We recognized that social media was not a necessity.

After the smartphone question, the next thing parents inevitably ask me is, "When should my child get social media?" Again, my answer is probably not going to make you happy. As the saying goes, sorry not sorry. Smartphones and social media are different because getting a smartphone can be a necessity, but social media isn't. It can be fun, and entertaining, introduce you to new things, help you plan a trip or make new friends or keep up with old ones, but that still doesn't make it a necessity. You can't even argue that it's necessary for business and self-promotion. My friend Erin Loechner, author of *The Opt-Out Family*, has proven this to be true by launching a book without any social media presence.

Social media is not a necessity for any child, but culture has led us to believe that having it is a rite of passage, or at least a rite of teenhood. Like author and activist Jonathan Haidt said, the concern is platforms designed to "keep the child's eyes glued to the screen for as long as possible in a never-ending stream of social comparison and validation-seeking from strangers"—platforms that see the user as the product, not the customer. Being different is seldom easy. But after watching my teens and many of their friends grow up without social media, I firmly believe it is the better way.

So instead of answering the question of when to let a child have social media with a hard-and-fast age, consider this idea: Give your child social media when you are ready for them to

- do a lot of scrolling,
- face potential addiction to that dopamine hit,
- deal with FOMO,
- see people being oversexualized and objectified,
- be propositioned by strangers or potential predators,
- compare themselves and their lives to others,
- stumble across porn,
- deal with the distraction of social media, and
- want whatever clothing or goods are trending.

I'm not saying all of these will happen when your child has social media. But some of them will. Because if we are being honest, we know some of these things have happened to us while on social media.

Tween and teen brains aren't emotionally developed to handle the temptation, distractions, and even danger that come with social media. It is a lot for even adults to handle. So wait as long as possible before giving your kids access. My goal for each of my children is that they wait until after high school. And when they do get social media, all the safeguards put in place for safe and responsible phone use are reviewed and implemented for social media too.

We built an offline life.

Above all, I'm advocating for us to offer our kids a rich offline life for many years before we hand them off to social media. We need to teach them the value of cultivating friendships and relationships in the real world. We need to help them engage in real-life activities with those friends. We need to let them feel discomfort and boredom and learn to do something positive with those feelings instead of numbing them with scrolling. They need to spend time talking to people face-to-face. They need to actually be social!

How often have I seen kids sitting next to each other at the bus stop or walking side by side, earbuds in and eyes on screen, not talking or engaging with one another and lost in an endless stream of memes, dances, and fifteen-second videos? No one is offering them help for engaging with one another.

How much better would it be to take those same teens out to a hiking trail and let them walk side by side where there is no internet to connect to and they have to watch their steps instead of a screen because the trail is rough and uneven? How much better to provide them the place and space to be social, to cultivate connection, and to grow relationships?

If you think teens aren't longing for real-life connection, consider this example: A couple years ago we had a birthday party for our second-oldest, William—a big group of teens and preteens hanging out on the beach for hours and hours. It was so much fun. I loved watching them play endless rounds of football, soccer, dodgeball, rugby, Spikeball, and who knows what other crazy games they invented. They reminded me of puppies—running, wrestling, playing, and loving the wild ruckus of it all.

One thing really stood out to me as I watched them play: None of them were on their phones. They were fully engaged in the moment and with one another. It was wonderful. When they stopped playing to eat, one of our son's buddies prayed for the meal. Here was part of his prayer: "Thank you for all these fun people who are here to celebrate William. And thank you that they actually like to play and not just sit around looking at their phones." Everyone clapped, cheered, and amen-ed, because they knew it was true.

Teens are longing for real-life connection away from screens. It's up to us to help them pursue it, find it, and create it. There are lots of ways to do this. You can put time limits on their phone use, keep them off social media, collect phones at the start of a get-together, or not give them a phone in the first place. I think all those strategies have their place. But what we've seen trump all those options is simply making screen-free activities so appealing that our kids desire to participate.

Instead of just imposing rules and restrictions, we're trying to create a family and community culture that creates and pursues real-life connection. We're trying to reach our kids' hearts, not just manage their behavior. This requires effort. It requires time. It requires creativity. It requires saying yes to things we might not love doing ourselves, but our kids do. It requires courage to step into their lives and engage with them, even when the culture says that's not what they want. Consider this my not-so-gentle nudge: Pursue connection with your kids! Help them create connections with their friends! Make sure they're finding connection in many areas of their lives.

HOW TO CREATE A UNIQUE FAMILY CULTURE

Here are ideas to create a family culture that is different from what the world is offering. Consider which ones speak to you and begin to implement them into your family life. When things need to change due to a child's growth and needs, be flexible and adapt as necessary. The goal is to create cultural norms that keep our kids as safe as possible, and as engaged in real life as possible, while learning to use tech responsibly.

Early years

- Extremely limit or allow no screen time before the age of three.
- Don't own a TV, or if you do, don't make it a central part of your home.
- Make screen time a treat for the whole family—Friday movie night or Saturday morning cartoons for the siblings.
- Don't give each child their own screen or device—they can listen to audiobooks together on a shared or family device.
- Draw on paper instead of screens.

- Use screens only in public spaces.
- Wait for video games until age thirteen.
- Use family computers and have them ask or inform parents before searching on Google.
- Don't make screens the default choice when friends come over to play.
- No screens in cars (try listening to books instead).
- Find out the screen rules at other homes before playdates, and if the home allows unmonitored screen time, invite the friend to your house instead.

Later years

- Don't play video games that are connected to the internet or have a chat capability.
- Give safe phones to kids only when really necessary.
- Give smartphones only when really, really necessary.
- Don't consume movies, TV shows, music videos, or video games that objectify people.
- Make accountability software and parental controls the norm for all devices.
- Wait on social media until the later teen years—the ideal is over eighteen or out of high school.
- Share passwords with the family—yours and theirs.

What tech culture do you want to create in your family? Start making it happen—you get to decide! Whether your kids are four or fourteen, you get to create this culture. The older the kids are, the bigger the adjustment will be, so put the changes into practice with grace, flexibility, and plenty of humor. Living a different life is worth it. You got this!

IT'S TIME TO REFLECT

- Think about your favorite screen-free activities from childhood. Can you introduce some of them to your kids?
- Are you ready to create a family culture that might look different from a lot of other people's? What part about that makes you nervous? What makes you excited?
- Can you think of any friends or families who might join you in this endeavor?
- Using the list in this chapter, what is one thing you can do this week to begin creating a community of like-minded parents and families?
- What is one thing from the list that you can do this week to begin creating a unique family culture?

TEN

Pursue Connection with Your Kids

Pornography pulls people away from each other because it's an easy escape from the hard work of real relationships. Matt Fradd says that "relationships can be complicated: they involve truly knowing, caring for, and serving another person at the expense of one's own desires. Pornography, however, is one-sided."[1] We know this is true because pornography is utterly devoid of connection. It is empty, isolating, and a truly lonely experience. Sex with a loving partner, as God designed it, has the capacity to be the most powerfully connecting act we'll ever experience. But a sexual act with an image on a screen has no connecting power at all.

Author and political activist Naomi Wolf has traveled all over the United States talking with college students about relationships. "When I ask about loneliness, a deep, sad silence descends on audiences of young men and young women alike," she says. "They know they are lonely together . . . and that [porn] is a big part of that loneliness. What they don't know is how to get out."[2] Parents! This is our wake-up call! We must show our kids that there is a different way. We must provide opportunities for connection.

If we want our kids to authentically connect with other people and eventually with their spouses, we have to live that out with them and provide the space for it to develop. We have to be proactive, at first creating real-life connections with our children and then helping them create those with others, like siblings and friends. This is an investment in their future health and happiness.

PARENTAL CONNECTION

The first connection we want to foster with our kids is their connection with us. One of the best ways to do this is to begin with a vision for long-term connection. We want to cultivate a lasting relationship with our kids. Did you know that's a countercultural idea? Society tells us that it's natural and normal for our kids to grow disconnected from us.

I remember my years as a mom of young kids. I'd be waddling through the grocery store, big and pregnant with a toddler and a couple preschoolers wandering around behind me. Nearly every time someone would stop me and say, "Look at your little crew. Aren't they just the sweetest?" And I'd smile and say thank you, knowing exactly what was coming next.

Sure enough, their tone would change from sweet to dark with foreboding: "But just you wait until they're teenagers. You're really going to have your hands full then!" Sometimes they'd tell me a story about their own horrible teenagers and how they missed the little years. Meanwhile my littles would be getting restless and at least one of them would be climbing something or hiding somewhere dangerous or filthy. It was a lot of fun.

Those moments in the store stirred up my rebellious heart

and prompted me to say, "That is not going to be our story!" I had a vision and purpose to write a different story with our family. We didn't have to become splintered and fractured with slamming doors and angry voices day in and day out as soon as we hit the teen years. Instead I dreamed that my kids would reach the teen years and they'd still be my favorite people.

Spoiler alert: As of writing this book, I have three teens and a young adult, and my dream has come true. They are indeed my most favorite people to hang out with, laugh with, have deep talks with, and adventure with. I absolutely adore them.

The teen years have had hard spots to be sure, but I could say the same for any part of parenting. What no one ever told me about the teen years is that besides being hard, they can also be incredibly, insanely wonderful.

Real, lasting connection isn't going to happen automatically or magically. I couldn't just wish for it. I had to be purposeful about modeling it, living it, and making space for it. I had to put in the work. Cultivating connection meant inviting my kids into relationship with me over and over again. I couldn't rely on the fact that we're related. That's not a guarantee that connection exists. We have to be intentional.

So after years of hearing the dire warnings from those dooms-day prophets at the grocery store, I decided it was time to make that vision of a different story for our family into reality. We'd already implemented plenty of choices as part of our family culture, but I wanted to add something that got us away from home and outside our routine. When I was away from home and the to-do list and all the things that made up my mental load, I was more able to be fully present with my kids. I realized I needed to carve out time and space to connect with them in a meaningful way.

For us that came in the form of weekly adventures. Almost every week we got away from the house—usually outside and away from cell service too—and spent time together. It's been sixteen years of these weekly investments in cultivating connection with my kids, and we're still loving it! Adventure was the vehicle, but connection was the goal.

Because the reality is, our kids are growing up in a world where they are experiencing more and more digital connection but less and less real-life connection with nature, books, and especially with people. Culture is offering a growing list of subpar replacements for real-life connections through TV shows, video games, social media, and virtual reality. It also offers dangerous substitutes for real connection through pornography.

Knowing this is the world my kids are growing up in, I recognized that we had to do more than pursue connections ourselves. We had to teach our kids how to recognize and to pursue them. Now more than ever we must teach our kids what real-life connection, intimacy, and healthy relationships look like so that they can distinguish them from the counterfeits. This is such important work. It might seem that simply hanging out with and enjoying our kids is not the hard work we need to do. But it is!

Cultivating connection will require work. It's more than just sitting side by side on the drive to school or soccer practice. It might look like this:

- Choosing conversation in the car instead of popping in earbuds.
- Listening to the same music or book in the car together or in the kitchen while prepping dinner.

- Inviting a kid along on a shopping trip or to run errands rather than going alone.
- Taking part in an activity, class, or project that they love and doing it with them.
- Staying up late to talk to, or listen to, your teen.
- Spending regular time together without the distraction of technology. Give them your eyes.

As parents, we crave a lasting relationship with our kids. We want them to want to be with us when they're toddlers, but also when they're teens, young adults, new parents, and for the rest of our lives. But teaching our kids how to build and maintain meaningful relationships isn't just about us. It's the foundation for all other relationships and helps them move into the next stages for friendship.

SIBLING AND FRIEND CONNECTIONS

We also need to help our kids build connections with their siblings and friends. *That's easy,* you're thinking. *They're always around their siblings.* But I'm talking about helping your kids learn to play together, talk to one another, and ultimately make heart-to-heart connections.

So many kids don't know how to be in real relationship because they're just sitting next to each other gaming or scrolling social media. I feel sad each time I see kids walking next to each other with earbuds in and their music playing instead of talking to each other. They're in each other's presence, yes, but they're not involved or invested in each other's lives.

There is an epidemic of loneliness among kids these days, especially teens. And there is a correlation between loneliness and how much time teens are spending on social media. "In the most recent data, 22% of 10th grade girls spend seven or more hours a day on social media . . . which means many teenage girls are doing little else than sleeping, going to school and engaging with social media. . . . Across the board, since 2010, anxiety, depression and loneliness have all increased."[3] This isn't the story I want for my kids or yours. I want our kids involved in the lives of their siblings and their friends.

I can recall the first time my daughter experienced this kind of isolation and loneliness with peers. We were attending a mother-daughter retreat for a weekend. It was a retreat we'd been to twice before, and both of us loved it. We didn't go with any friends and made new friends every time. This year my daughter was moving up from the ten-and-under class to the next age group. She was excited for new crafts and activities and more meaningful discussions during Bible study time.

Knowing this, I was surprised by her downcast attitude as we walked back to our cabin after the first night. "Hey! How was your group tonight? Was it fun? Did you make any new friends?" She shook her head and said in a disheartened voice, "Everyone had a phone. And all they wanted to do was be on them." I was shocked. She was only eleven. The other girls were also eleven and twelve. Could this be happening already? Tween girls choosing their phones over real-life connection, real-life fun, and real-life friendship? It *was* happening, and my daughter was the one paying the price.

For some parents this might have been the moment they say, "I guess you're at that age now. It's time to get you a phone!" And some kids would walk away from that moment convinced that they needed a phone to fit in and find friends—albeit online ones. But that was not my response or my daughter's. This experience only made me more determined to offer my girl, and my boys, as many real-life connection opportunities as I could. And my daughter, who had a life rich in real-life friendships, felt the same way. She didn't want to hang out with people who spent all their time looking at a screen, taking selfies, or practicing TikTok dances. She craved the quality of connection and friendship she'd known her whole life.

Giving our kids that connection with family and friends requires an investment of our time, energy, and often finances and other resources. It's often a lot of work and—especially as my kids have gotten older—often requires me to stay up late because they have friends over or need a ride home from a friend's house. Or I stay up late to hear about the party they were at or what they did while they were out for the night with friends. But I'll say again and again that *it is worth it*. Watching and hearing about their friendships flourishing is worth every late night and all the money I spend filling the gas tank.

What does this look like to invest in our kids' relationships with friends? Here are some ideas:

- Commit to making time in your schedule and routine to have their friends over to visit.
- Take your kids and their friends hiking. Not only is there often no cell service on a trail, but walking together shoulder to shoulder provides a perfect backdrop for real conversation.
- Set up regular playdates with your kids' friends. One way is through a babysitting trade. Watch your friend's kids one afternoon and the next week she'll watch yours. This gives each mom a break and the kids get a playdate out of it.

- Let your garage be the place where the band practices or where the workout equipment lives, and let your kitchen be the place where your kids and their friends can bake cakes and decorate them.
- Be okay with having a messy house before or after kids come over.
- As your kids get older, be the house with the best food. Nothing draws in teenagers like food.
- Be quick to say yes when your kid asks, "Can I invite everyone over for a hangout / Bible study / backyard movie night / sleepover / game night?" Let them know they can count on you.
- Be the one to drive. You'll get to listen and talk with them about the important things in their lives.

We absolutely must provide space and time for our kids to connect with us, with their siblings, and with their friends free from screens. Yes, this requires more effort. It will take more of our time, resources, and energy. It might make our homes louder, messier, and more chaotic. But *this is an antidote to pornography use* and to pornography addiction. It is our chance to say to our kids, "God has something so much better planned for you, and I am here to help you experience it." My children and their future are worth all of that. Yours are too.

IT'S TIME TO REFLECT

- Did you grow up in a family where you felt truly connected to your parents and siblings, or did it feel more like you were just people who lived together?

- If you felt a strong sense of connection, what did your family do to cultivate those connections?
- If you weren't very connected to your family, what are a few ways you can intentionally cultivate connection with your children and begin to write a new story for your family?
- How can you make space for cultivating your children's friendships? List at least two ideas and make them happen this week.
- Plan a family outing or activity that will cultivate connection for all of you.
- If you have or have had a child who is dealing with loneliness, how can you help them cultivate connection with family first and then with friends?
- Talk as a family about loneliness and how modern-day people are struggling to connect with others. Then brainstorm ways to create connection in the midst of loneliness.

PART THREE

The Hardest
Questions

ELEVEN

What Do I Do After My Child Has Seen Porn?

It's what every parent dreads and the message I get every week: "My child has been exposed to pornography. I feel sick. I am devastated. What do I do?"

The details vary—confessed or discovered, accidental exposure or sought out, at a friend's house or at home, younger child or older teen, on an unlocked device or fully protected one—but the end result is always the same: devastated, heartbroken parents and a struggling child.

This doesn't have to be the end of the story. There is hope and healing available for your child, and it starts with you. Your posture in this moment makes a tremendous difference in how your child will process this event. My friend Chris McKenna of Protect Young Eyes says our kids need to know they can always "land safely and softly with us." When we are able to offer that kind of landing for our kids, no matter how we're feeling about it, it sets them on the path of healing much faster.

In chapter 8 I shared a story of the time one of our kids watched a Super Bowl half-time show and was exposed to soft porn. The way I responded to that situation is exactly how I'd respond to one of our kids seeing pornography. But because seeing explicit pornography would be even more emotionally charged than seeing soft porn, I am sharing here, step by step, what you can do when you learn your child has seen pornography.

Note: It is valuable to read through this chapter before a pornography exposure takes place so that you can be prepared. In the same way your child needs a porn plan, you as a parent need a plan, except that your plan is all about how you'll respond to them. Begin praying in advance that God will give you a calm heart, a facial expression that conveys love and compassion, a gentle spirit toward them in their moment of need, and a clear head that remembers what to say.

Above all, please remember that while the discovery of porn exposure or porn use hurts our hearts, God can use us to bring healing and comfort to our child whose heart is also hurting. Now more than ever, may we be instruments of God's peace.

1. PROCESS YOUR OWN EMOTIONS

The first thing to understand is that it is absolutely normal for you, the parent, to experience a cascade of different emotions. You might feel angry, sad, disappointed, afraid, horrified, ashamed, and overwhelmed in the course of an hour or a few days. Those emotions are valid and do not make you a bad parent. It is also important to remember the words of Psalm 34:18: "The LORD is close to the brokenhearted and saves those who are crushed in spirit." God cares about your heart in this matter. And he cares about your child. He cares even more than you do.

That's why, in the wake of discovery, you need to summon every ounce of self-control, compassion, love, and grace the Holy Spirit grants you and pour those out on your child instead of the other emotions you feel. You want to offer shame-free warmth and care. Make sure they know that they are not in trouble. There's time later to talk of setting up new boundaries and guardrails. Now is not the time for that. Now is the time to be near your child both physically and emotionally.

2. CONNECT WITH THEM

After confession or discovery, if your child is open to it, hug them, hold them, or at least be physically near to them. Your job is to help them feel safe, peaceful, and even happy again. Pray together that God can take the pictures out of their mind and bring them healing. That should be the whole of the first conversation. You can let them know there is more to talk about later, but that is all you need to talk about now. It is not the right time for a lengthy lecture or even conversation. Be loving and be brief. You'll be back to talk more later.

3. TAKE TIME TO PREPARE FOR THE CONVERSATION

The reason it is ideal to wait for the next conversation is because it is going to be more awkward and potentially painful. You need to determine the extent of your child's exposure. If they confessed to you, you'll be asking questions to see if this was a one-time viewing or if they went back to see more. If possible you'll want to look at the history of the device used to get a clear picture of the trauma your child might be walking through based on what they were exposed to.

If your child didn't come to you and you made the discovery, chances are you already know what they saw. But it's still important to find out how long they have been viewing pornography, where, etc. It's also helpful to encourage them to share with you if they can, as this helps release some of the pain and guilt and shame they are dealing with. Reassure your child that your questions are for their healing and safety, not because they are in trouble.

4. APPROACH THE CONVERSATION WITH KINDNESS

If your child is old enough to know that pornography and sex are connected, you need to let them know that pornography is not how God designed sex to be. You can tell them that God designed sex to be safe, loving, and in the context of marriage. This is not what they saw, and they need you to help them know the truth.

Your child might be filled with remorse and willing to talk and confess. They might be confused. It is common for younger adolescents and children to say they don't know why they went back to look at the pictures and videos. They know it didn't make them feel good to look, but it was hard to stop looking.

For an older child, especially one who didn't confess but was caught, you might face more anger and sullenness or less willingness to talk. This is normal, and that child needs compassion just as much as the one who willingly confesses everything. Wherever your child falls on this spectrum, try to get as much information from them as possible, check devices if you can, pray together again, and save the next part of this ongoing conversation for later.

5. HOW TO MOVE FORWARD

The next talk you need to have with your child is about the steps you'll be taking to keep them safe from further pornography exposure. Explain you must change the rules with devices in your home to keep them safe.

Now is the time to change passwords, turn on all the parental controls if you haven't yet, and only allow them to use tech with supervision. If they were seeking out porn, consider installing monitoring software like Bark and accountability software like Covenant Eyes on all family-owned devices.

For some kids these changes will be a relief. For others it will feel like a punishment, and they may be upset or angry. You'll have to stand your ground and do what is best for your child in the long run instead of making them happy in the here and now. Look for all the ways your child could get online, such as video game consoles, old phones, computers, and tablets. Clear your house of those things to protect your child. If they are young and mostly accessing the internet at home through your Wi-Fi, consider installing a router to help stop problematic content.

Finally, it is time to begin filling your child's mind, heart, and life with the antidote to the evil they consumed. Spend the next days, weeks, and months filling their mind with all kinds of good things to help replace the bad.

- Read beautiful and wholesome stories and picture books together.
- Fill your house with hymns and worship music.
- Read and memorize Scripture together. Start with 2 Corinthians 5:17: "Therefore, if anyone is in Christ, the new creation has come: The old has gone, the new is here!"
- Write Scripture on cards and put them all over your house.
- Spend time outdoors as often as possible.
- Be with friends who bring joy and delight to your child's life.
- Make extra effort to cultivate connection with your child and to provide opportunities for them to connect to God, His creation, and His people.

Also consider if your child needs help beyond what you can offer. If they were accidentally exposed to pornography and did not continue to seek it out, you are probably capable of helping them heal. But if your child was actively using porn for a time and especially if they did not confess and were discovered, you might want to get them extra support from a pastor or counselor.

It is of utmost importance that you seek out help from someone who has knowledge and training in recovery from porn and sex addiction as well as an understanding of brain neuroplasticity. If your local church cannot help you in this area, seek help through a counseling center or look for help online. See the Resource Guide in the back of this book for a list of suggested organizations.

Your child may not feel comfortable or willing to talk to

someone else about what has happened. Communicate that this person knows how to help them heal, and you will be there to offer any support you can. Be loving but firm if this is the step they need in healing.

TALKING TO YOUR KIDS AFTER PORNOGRAPHY EXPOSURE

CONVERSATION 1: DISCOVERING THE EXPOSURE

Key concept

I love you. I'm here to help you and keep you safe.

Sample dialogue

I'm so sorry for what you saw. I wish I could have kept you safe from that. Right now I know you might be feeling a lot of different things—scared, confused, sad, angry. Those feelings are normal. Let's pray that God will take those pictures out of your mind and bring you healing.

CONVERSATION 2: INFORMATION GATHERING

1. Determine the extent of your child's exposure. Reassure your child that your questions are for their healing and safety, not because they are in trouble.
2. Get as much information from them as possible.

3. Check the devices to see what was accessed if possible.
4. Pray together.
5. Save the next part of this ongoing conversation for later.

CONVERSATION 3: NEXT STEPS

Key concept

We're changing the rules with devices in our home to keep you safe.

Additional key concept for older kids

God designed sex to be safe, loving, and in the context of marriage.

It is tempting to give into despair when walking through this situation, which can be one of the most challenging in modern parenting. But you are not alone. So many other parents have walked the exact same road.

There is so much fear and shame attached to pornography that few parents are talking about it. We don't want anyone to think badly of our child or of us as parents. But we need to band together to create a safer, more supportive world for our kids and for one another. Seeing porn is not to be the end of your child's story.

TWELVE

How Do I Talk About Masturbation with My Kids?

"What about masturbation?" This might be the number one question I get from parents. They're often uncomfortable to ask me about it, but they're even more uncomfortable talking to their kids—they need help. For years I avoided bringing up masturbation because let's be real: masturbation is awkward and very personal to talk about. But the biggest reason I found it challenging to address is that I've been hurt by it.

Porn use is almost always coupled with masturbation, so masturbation had been a big piece of the damaged parts of our marriage. I didn't know if I could talk about it without letting my own hurt cloud my thoughts or just breaking down altogether. But after a good amount of time passed and a lot of healing took place, I decided to swallow my fears and face the question so many parents were asking me.

Masturbation could impact the future sexual health and well-being of a child, so it deserves attention. Also, just like the other topics in this book, if parents aren't equipped to talk with their kids about this, those kids could get their answers from their friends, popular culture, or the internet.

THE DIFFERENCE BETWEEN SELF-STIMULATION AND MASTURBATION

The first thing every parent needs to understand is the difference between a child who is prepuberty and self-stimulating and a preteen or teen who is masturbating. Young children who are self-stimulating are not engaging in a sexual act. They are just doing something that they've discovered feels good. But once they've discovered it feels good, they could then use this act of self-stimulating as a way of coping with uncomfortable feelings like frustration, boredom, anxiety, fatigue, or stress. They won't realize that they're doing this, but as parents we should be aware so we can teach them better coping tools.

I engaged in self-stimulation as a child, and for me it was simply a self-soothing activity just like sucking my thumb or stroking my blankie. I didn't connect it to sex because I was young and had no idea what sex even was. It wasn't until I was a preteen and learned about masturbation from the book my mom gave me, *Preparing for Adolescence*, that I realized the self-soothing I'd done as a child was connected.

During my teen years, masturbation did not become an addictive habit or my coping mechanism for difficult emotions. But if it had, I'd have been walking through it by myself because I don't remember my parents ever talking to me about mastur-bation. The same was true for my husband. Like many of you, we both grew up in an era when these topics were seldom, if ever, talked about. I don't think our parents were ever given the tools to have these discussions with their kids. But in an effort to create more openness with our kids about sexual things, we wanted this topic to be one of the many we discussed with them.

NORMAL, HARMLESS, AND HEALTHY?

The typical cultural view of masturbation is that everyone does it and it's no big deal. It is the source of lots of jokes, and there are also lots of stories recounting the negative things that could happen to a person who does not masturbate. The view presented by most experts in the health field is that masturbation is normal, harmless, and even healthy. They'll rarely mention any negatives associated with it, which I don't think is entirely honest.

In Christian circles masturbation is seldom talked about. If it is, it's usually deemed wrong without any explanation on why it's considered sinful or why a teen would engage in that behavior. I believe we need to talk to our kids about masturbation instead of ignoring it or pretending it doesn't happen. Neither of those options helps our kids move toward a healthy sexual future.

Consider some ideas about masturbation and the impact it could have on a child's sexual future. I am not saying these things will happen to your child if they engage in masturbation. However, this information is worth thinking about since it's not the typical you'll hear presented in secular or even Christian circles. You need to come to your own conclusions about masturbation so you can comfortably talk to your kids about it.

Some ideas to consider about masturbation:

Masturbation distorts God's design for intimacy. Sexual intimacy is designed for two people. It is the most intimate and connecting act we can engage in. When we turn sexual intimacy into a solitary act, we make it only about pleasing ourselves. That is not what God designed sex for.

Masturbation can be an unhealthy way to deal with negative emotions. It's very common to turn to masturbation when experiencing feelings of boredom, sadness, stress, loneliness, depression, or a poor self-image. That's because masturbation releases a big hit of the feel-good chemical dopamine, which takes care of those negative feelings for a while. The trouble is, masturbation doesn't deal with the source of those feelings. It simply masks or dulls them for a short time. Masking negative emotions with masturbation is just as unhealthy as masking them with things like binge eating, drug or alcohol abuse, compulsive shopping, or mindless scrolling.

Masturbation promotes objectification of others. It is common to engage in masturbation while fantasizing about another person. Often those fantasies are not honoring to those people. Instead, those fantasies take people from their true role as people worthy of honor and respect and turn them into sex objects to be used for our own pleasure.

Masturbation can lead to sexual selfishness in marriage. While marriage may feel far off for our children, we are doing our best to set up our children for a lifetime of sexual health and wholeness. Therefore, it is good to consider how masturbation could impact the health of their marriage one day. For example, one spouse has been used to masturbating for years and still prefers that sexual activity to engaging in a sacrificial, loving relationship that requires putting the other person's needs and desires first.

Masturbation can be selfish and contribute to avoidance instead of dealing with the root issues in a sexual relationship.

When coupled with porn, masturbation can become a mentally, physically, and emotionally damaging habit. Science is only beginning to show the full impact that porn consumption has on the brain and body. However, research does already show that regular porn use can contribute to things like depression, marital dissatisfaction, disinterest in regular activities, viewing people as objects to be used for personal gain, self-hatred, intimacy disorders, and even erectile dysfunction in otherwise healthy young men. When porn use is coupled with masturbation, it can become a very difficult habit to break, and for some people it can lead to porn addiction or sexual addiction. That is because "masturbation while viewing pornography cements an attachment to pornography because that is what sexual release is intended to do: create a bond to what we are looking at during sexual stimulation."[1]

Take some time to sit with these ideas and decide what you believe about each one. Since masturbation is seldom talked about outside of jokes or the cultural view that it is normal and healthy, I may have introduced you to some new ideas. They might feel uncomfortable. You might disagree with some or all of them. That's okay! My goal is to help you determine your own thoughts and beliefs on this topic so you can help your kids grow toward healthy sexual maturity. I invite you to pray about this, talk about it with your spouse, and then make a plan for how you want to talk about it with your kids.

When kids are young and we notice self-stimulating activities, it is really important not to overreact. We don't want to punish our child for this behavior because we don't want to shame them. "Shame is the primary driver in addiction and the last thing we want our child to associate with any part of their sexuality."[2] Instead, we just redirect them toward a new activity. That is as simple as picking them up and saying, "Let's read a book together!" Or, "You look like you need to get up and move around. Let's play chase!"

If we think our child is tired, hungry, bored, or sad, we can address those emotions and meet those needs. "Are you feeling tired? Come cuddle on the couch with me." Or "You seem sad. Want to tell me about it while we color some pictures?" Redirecting is not a punishment; it's simply a way to help our kids do something different. Even more important, we're beginning to teach them how to manage those negative feelings in a positive and healthy way.

When kids become developmentally able to understand the idea of handling negative emotions in a positive way (probably the preteen years), and we notice they're still engaging in self-stimulating activities, we can have a short and simple conversation.

Again, we don't make it about shame or make them feel bad for engaging in self-stimulation. Instead, it's just about treating their body and emotions in the best way possible.

Around the ages of ten to twelve—or earlier if your child is one who starts puberty at a younger age—puberty discussions should begin. We need to discuss with our preteen all the ways their body, brain, and emotions are changing or are going to change. This is a good time to explain that masturbation is something more than just an activity that simply feels good. You might feel really uncomfortable having this conversation, but this is an opportunity to guide your child on a path toward a healthy sexual future. This is a way for you to love and care for them. Be honest and avoid shaming and negativity.

In the beginning you don't need to go into great detail or

make this conversation very long. You could let them ask questions if they have any. They might not because of the personal nature of the topic. But if they do, answer them honestly. Over the next months and years, as they are developmentally ready, you can continue to talk about masturbation.

Like most conversations I talk about in this book, this is not a one-and-done conversation. It needs to be ongoing and even organic. That means not sitting everyone down on the couch and saying, "Let's talk about masturbation!" Because that would probably feel really awkward.

Instead, aim for something more like this: While you're already hanging out, driving, or going for a walk, start with, "Hey, I wanted to talk to you about something . . ." It's good to check in with our kids now and then and see if they're struggling with anything sexually or have questions about anything sexual. Masturbation could be one of those things.

We can also respond to situational moments, like seeing an explicit billboard or show, by having a conversation about how it makes them feel or how they handle seeing something like that. I initiate these conversations because I want my kids to know that I care about every part of them. I want the very best for them in every part of their life, including their emotional and sexual health.

There is no one right way to have these conversations. Sometimes we have had them with a couple of kids at once and sometimes they take place one on one. Sometimes they have been mom to son, or dad to daughter because we have worked hard to create a very safe and open culture in our family where we can discuss anything. Most often though, the conversations are mom to daughter and father to son because we can identify with one another's journeys in more specific ways.

In our family, we were also honest about our own journey with masturbation. There is no need to go into detail, but it can help our kids to know we've dealt with this issue just like they are. Make it very clear every time you talk about masturbation that this is not about shame or guilt, but to offer them something better. Because the truth is that God's design for intimacy is best and so much better than masturbation.

If you feel like you simply can't have these conversations with your child and there is no other parent to step in, please seek out a trusted friend to invest in relationship with your child and then invite them into the conversation. These topics are too important to take a pass on, so I urge you to figure out an alternative if you can't engage in the conversation yourself.

TALKING TO YOUR KIDS ABOUT MASTURBATION

YOUNGER KIDS

Redirect toward a new activity. Begin to teach them how to manage negative feelings in a positive and healthy way.

OLDER KIDS

Sample dialogue

Hey sweetie, I see you're rubbing your private parts, and I know that it can feel good to do that. Sometimes people do this because they are tired, bored, mad, hungry, or upset. But that is not the best way for us to deal with those feelings. So if you are feeling those things, you don't have to hide from those emotions. Instead, you can talk to me and to God and we'll help you. God made your body and your mind, and we want to treat all of you in the best way possible.

PRETEENS AND TEENS

Sample dialogue

Sweetheart, I want to talk to you about something called masturbation. Masturbation is when you touch or rub your private parts. You might do this because you are curious about those parts of your body. You might even discover that it feels good when you do this.

You are not strange or bad if you masturbate, but it can become a problem in your life if it becomes a habit. This usually happens when you masturbate because you are having unpleasant emotions like embarrassment, frustration, or sadness. There are better ways to deal with those emotions than through masturbation, and I will help you learn what those better ways are. Remember, God cares about every part of you, and he wants you to find the best ways to take care of yourself.

Frequent or compulsive masturbation is not good for you. Masturbation combined with pornography can be addictive and harmful, but God's plan for sexuality is bigger and better than masturbation! God designed sex for a person and their spouse, and therefore it is best to wait for God's best.

THIRTEEN

How Do I Talk About Nudity in Art with My Kids?

Nudity and art is a complex conversation, especially in a world saturated with pornography. I get asked about this topic often, especially by art-loving families. They don't want to expose their kids to pornography but also don't want to give up on going to the art museum or thumbing through art books.

Here's the truth: There is no one-size-fits-all answer. In fact, some of you will disagree with my thoughts here. Every family must decide how they'll approach nudity and art. I hope this will give you helpful ideas as you cultivate a healthy sexual culture in your family.

My kids can ask me any question and I will answer as calmly and lovingly as I can.

As the kids matured, our conversations have gotten deeper and become more complex and nuanced. But starting with these basic but important concepts gave them a solid foundation. Like many of our conversations, this one happened organically when we were visiting an art museum together.

The kids were around the ages of seven, five, three, and one and loving our museum trip. When they saw a nude statue right near a painting featuring the Bible character Lazarus, one of them asked, "Why is there a naked statue and a Bible character right next to each other? Do those go together?"

I took this opportunity to remind them that in the garden of Eden, Adam and Eve were naked. I wanted my kids to understand that the human body wasn't something to be embarrassed by or afraid of. The human body didn't need to be a source of shame or any kind of bad feelings. But it was also the perfect opportunity to give the kids a simple lesson on discernment. That is, listening to the voice inside them when it says, "That makes me feel uncomfortable" and then acting on those feelings.

YOUNGER KIDS

It can feel challenging to teach young kids about nudity and art because they're more likely to see things as black and white. If we've said, "No clothes equals pornography," they might yell "Pornography!" when we're at an art museum. Or they might be confused when they study art for school and see nudes in a textbook. This is why I had that first conversation with my kids about nudity and art. I wanted them to be able to discern that a painting of a mother breastfeeding a child is probably not pornography. I wanted them to understand and begin practicing discernment.

You can use the above conversation as a guide for a conversation with your own kids. If they are younger, you'll want to keep it simple, telling them they can look away or walk away from art that makes them uncomfortable. You can teach them the word "discernment," too, so from a young age they are familiar with what it is and practice it.

OLDER KIDS

With older kids the conversations surrounding nudity and art can become more complex. For example, you can discuss the purpose of pornography versus the purpose of art. But you can still use that conversation I had with my kids as your starting place.

The conversation should keep growing as our kids do because they're growing up in a complex time. None of us knows exactly how to do this best because so much of it is new. Therefore, cover these conversations in prayer before they even happen. Seek God's wisdom and guidance above all else. He cares about your kids even more than you do!

TALKING TO YOUR KIDS ABOUT NUDITY IN ART

YOUNGER KIDS

Key concept
1. Your body is wonderfully made by God and designed with purpose.
2. The human body is worthy of respect and honor.
3. Your body, brain, and heart can tell you when something doesn't feel safe or good.

Sample dialogue

Child: Why is there a naked statue and a Bible character right next to each other? Do those go together?

Parent: God made them that way. They were made in
his image and their bodies were not shameful or
bad. Some pieces of art celebrate and honor the
human body. They remind us that the body is an
incredible machine designed by a God who loves
us and created each part of our body for a purpose. But there are other pieces of art that don't
celebrate, honor, or respect the human body. And
when we see them, we might get an uncomfortable
or yucky feeling. If that happens to you, it is okay to
look away or to say, "I don't want to look at that!"

When you have those thoughts or feelings,
that is your heart talking to you. Some people call
it your intuition. I believe it can be the Holy Spirit
letting you know this is something that is not good
for you and guiding you to something better. It is
good to recognize the yucky or uncomfortable feelings and respond to them instead of pretending
they aren't there. This is called discernment, and
it is important to be a discerning person. It helps
us determine right from wrong and safety from
danger. So remember, there are many beautiful
pieces of art that celebrate, respect, and honor the
human body. But there are others that do not. We

have the power to discern when a piece of art feels right or wrong to us. And if it feels bad, we have the power to look away or walk away.

OLDER KIDS

Use above content for younger kids as a starting point.

Sample dialogue

Even in artwork the human body is worthy of respect and honor because humans are God's children and beloved by Him. You can and should practice discernment when looking at art. If a piece feels difficult or uncomfortable, even if it's a piece that honors and celebrates the human body, you are free to take a pass and move on. I'll support you and honor that decision and move on with you because you matter more to me than the piece of art ever could.

FOURTEEN

How Do I Talk About Sexting, Nudes, and Sextortion with My Kids?

Despite the danger and harm that come from sexting and sending nudes, it is becoming more and more socially acceptable for young adults, teens, and even middle schoolers to get involved in it. Sexting is sending, receiving, or forwarding sexually explicit messages, photos, or videos via text or through social media apps, messaging apps, gaming sites or consoles, or email. Sexting is also called "sending nudes" or "sexts." Nudes are naked or semi-naked images sent online. Because of the devastating and dangerous outcomes that can occur from sexting, it is absolutely imperative that parents talk to their kids about these activities.

Even if your kid doesn't have a phone, they are not immune to this issue. They can see nudes a friend sends or receives on their phone. They can face requests for nudes or sextortion via video games or through email. Kids without phones are still at risk because we live in a world saturated in technology. We wish we could put our kids in a bubble and protect them from all of this, that we'd never have to say a thing about these terrible things happening out in the world, but that will not prepare our kids for life.

By middle school, parents need to talk to their kids about the dangers of sexting and give them a plan for what to do if or when it happens to them. If your child is already in high school or even college and you haven't discussed these topics with them, you still need to. Because for many kids and teens, getting asked for a nude photo is a measure of popularity or attractiveness. And there is immense peer pressure and social normalization to encourage kids to engage in sexting. Adolescent brains are still developing and don't fully understand the risks—especially when our culture is telling them sexting is fun and harmless. The reality, though, is altogether different. So be brave and know you're doing what's best for your kiddo.

TALKING TO YOUR KIDS ABOUT NUDES AND SEXTING

AGES 10+

Key concept
Nudes are naked or semi-naked images sent online—most often through text, but they can also be sent through video games or even email.

Sample dialogue
Has anyone ever asked you for a nude or sent you

one? Sending nudes and sexting might seem normal for kids your age, but it is also really dangerous and can get you into disastrous situations.

I know this conversation feels really awkward. I totally understand how you're feeling, but we have to talk about it because your safety is so important. Let's talk about some of the dangers you could face in participating in sexting.

Did you know that sending or receiving sexually explicit material of anyone under the age of eighteen is considered child pornography / child sexual abuse material and is against the law?

Once a nude is sent to someone, it can be saved and shared with others. When the photo or video leaves your phone or computer, you have no control over where it goes. Even a photo sent on a social media app that has disappearing software can be screenshot and saved.

Kids who have their explicit images shared online often experience crippling shame, anxiety, fear, depression, and even suicidal thoughts and ideations. Some of these kids even take their own life.

If you've already sent nudes or sexted, I'm not angry with you. But I want to make sure you don't continue to do it because it's not safe. And if you haven't sent nudes before or asked for them, let's talk about what to do if a situation arises where someone does ask you to send or receive them.

> ## OLDER TEENS
>
> Additional information to cover with high schoolers
>
> **Sample dialogue**
> Males sometimes send nudes called "dick pics" (pictures of an erect penis) to show that they are interested in someone—or simply to harass them. It is common for these pictures to be sent to a female without her consent. Even when sexts are consensual, the images can be shared online or sent to others without the consent of the person in the picture or video. Sometimes this is called "revenge porn." This is always a risk when sharing intimate images or words.

STARTING THE CONVERSATION

This conversation should be honest and to the point. You can start by asking, "Has anyone ever asked you for a nude or sent you one?"

If they're young (ten to twelve years old), they might look confused and not know what you're talking about. So you give them a definition of what a nude is. If they're older and roll their eyes and say, "Mooom!" then they know exactly what you're talking about. Then you carry on with the conversation.

There is a strong possibility that your kid is going to feel really uncomfortable talking about this with you. That is okay! You can even acknowledge their discomfort and be compassionate. But don't let their discomfort keep you from having this conversation. Let them know it is too important to ignore.

There is a lot of information you can share about why sexting and sending nudes is dangerous. Since your kids are growing up in a culture that normalizes it, you need to be very clear about the dangers they face when sexting and sending nudes. Don't dance around the issue. Be specific about what can happen. You can read them the script verbatim, or you can engage with them by asking if they can think of any reasons why sexting and sending nudes is dangerous. Whatever they don't come up with on their own, you can make sure you cover with your list.

I know the list is heavy, and it might feel scary to share with your child. But consider the potential harm you are saving them from. I believe it is worth having the heavy conversation to keep your child safe.

Of course this conversation with a middle schooler is going to look different than with a high school senior. For example, I probably would not talk to my sixth grader about dick pics, but I would for sure talk about them with my high school senior. With a sixth grader, talking about nude or semi-nude pictures is probably going to be enough. But as the parent, you have to make those judgment calls because you are the one who knows your kid best. If they are in an environment where they might encounter dick pics, talk to them about it. The goal is to have these conversations with our kids before they face these dangers.

The next part of the conversation is to help your child know all the ways they can avoid becoming involved in sexting and sending nudes. I always try to invite my kids to contribute in these conversations by asking questions like "Can you think of any ways you can avoid sexting or sending nudes or having them sent to you? Let's brainstorm some ideas together."

If you have multiple children close in age, I find it's nice to have these conversations together. It takes some of the pressure off one child having to bear all the weight of the conversation, and it also builds a sense of camaraderie: "We're all in this together and facing it together." I think group discussions also create a culture in your home in which siblings know they can talk to one another as well as their parents about these difficult topics. So whether you're having this conversation with one child or multiple, create that list together of ways they can stay away from sexting. You can use the list in the script for reference.

And don't assume your kids will reject any limits you suggest in social media, technology, or phones. Sometimes kids are aware of the danger and they want help getting out. Or they see technology as a giant distraction and are looking for an escape. When you suggest these ideas, make sure they know these are all ideas and not things you're going to enforce right now. The point is not coming down on them with an iron fist but inviting them into the process of protecting themselves and making wise choices.

TALKING TO YOUR KIDS ABOUT AVOIDING SEXTING

AGES 10+

Sample dialogue:

Can you think of any ways you can avoid sexting or sending nudes or having them sent to you? Let's brainstorm some ideas together. Remember that these are all just ideas and not things we're going to enforce right now. Are there any things on this list that you're already doing or want to add?

Sample List of Ideas

- Tell your parents what social media apps you're on, and let them see who you are communicating with. (There might be pushback on this one. It's worth the fight.)
- Never communicate with strangers online, through texting, or through video games.
- Install software and apps on phones and other devices that look for dangerous online behavior and alert your parents when it occurs. (Find a list of these in the Resource Guide.)
- Don't give your phone number or email address to people you don't know. If you really need to give them something, give them your parent's info.
- Change the settings on your phone so you can't receive pictures from strangers via file sharing or AirDrop. (This happened to me on an airplane once. Every female on the plane whose phone was not set to private got a text at the same time from an unknown number. I didn't open it, but I could guess what it was.)
- Try using a safe phone—one that can't send or receive photos or access the internet.
- Delay beginning use of social media and messaging apps for as long as possible. When you absolutely

must use them, make sure your profile is set to private and never respond to direct messages from strangers.

- Remember that sexting can occur on gaming sites or through gaming consoles too. Don't play games where strangers can contact you.

The last part of the conversation will be what to do when sexting happens. For some kids this will all be supposition because it hasn't happened to them yet. But for others who've experienced it, they need this information just as much.

Remember, if your child confesses to sexting in any capacity, be loving and nonjudgmental in your response. The priority is to get them the help they need based on the severity of the situation. The talk about boundaries and accountability around tech can be a conversation you have in the future—the near future, but still the future. In this moment, focus on loving them, helping them, and doing whatever you need to keep them safe.

TALKING TO YOUR KIDS WHO'VE BEEN INVOLVED IN SEXTING

AGES 10+

Key concept

I will be with you to help you through this and help keep you safe.

Let's look at this list of what to do if you've been

involved in sexting. Can you think of anything to add to this?

- The most important thing to do if someone sends you a nude or asks for one is to *tell your parents*. They need to know right away so they can contact the correct person to help in the situation.
- If a sexually explicit photo or video of you has been shared online, you can take steps to try to get it taken down. Get help from the National Center for Missing and Exploited Children: https://takeitdown.ncmec.org.
- Don't continue to communicate with the person. If they keep messaging, show your parents and they'll know what to do.

SEXTORTION: THE BIGGEST DANGER

The gravest danger that comes from sexting and sending nudes is sextortion, and like sexting, it is incredibly important that you talk to your kids about it. The FBI defines sextortion as "a serious crime that occurs when someone threatens to distribute your private and sensitive material if you don't provide them images of a sexual nature, sexual favors, or money."[1] Sextortion most commonly occurs on social media apps.

It seems unimaginable that this could happen to one of our kids, but in the past few years sextortion has grown into an overwhelming problem around the world.[2] Children and adolescents are often the victims because they are easy prey due to their age and vulnerability. That means your kids need to know what sextortion is, how to avoid it, and what to do if it happens to them, because they are a target.

A couple of years ago I got an email that threatened me with sextortion. I hadn't taken or sent anyone explicit photos. But this particular scam said they'd installed software on my computer that could see every website I visited, and they knew I looked at lots of porn. If I didn't pay them money, they'd share this humiliating information with everyone I knew.

I saw right away that this was a scam, but I still felt vulnerable and ill at ease reading that email. I shared it with my kids because I wanted them to know that anyone can be a target. We talked about what else they needed to know about sextortion, starting with fully understanding the dangers.

In the same way you started the conversation about sexting and sending nudes, you need to talk about sextortion. Be straightforward. Your kids will probably be able to figure out some of the dangers on their own, but you can refer to the facts listed in the script to make sure they fully understand the risks.

The crucial part of this conversation is giving your kids the knowledge and tools to respond to sextortion. This is helpful for prevention and for those who've already experienced it. We want our kids to be equipped to deal with these dangerous people.

Just like the conversations about sexting, present this information to your kids with love and the assurance that you will walk through it with them and help them. I suggest sharing the list in the script with your kids and spending time talking through each item. We want them to have absolute clarity about what to do if they are ever facing sextortion.

TALKING TO YOUR KIDS ABOUT SEXTORTION

AGES 10+

Sample dialogue

Hey, I was wondering if you know anything about sextortion? It's a very serious crime. Someone threatens to share your private and very personal material if you don't give them sexual images or videos, or do sexual acts, or give them money. It's a kind of blackmail.

Here are some facts about the dangers of sextortion:

- Children and adolescents are targets for sextortion, but the number one target is teen males.
- Sometimes sextortion happens over a long period of time. The predator will pretend to be a friend to get you to send them photos and videos. This is called "grooming."
- But sometimes sextortion happens with almost no grooming. It can be as simple as a sexually explicit message or image sent and one asked for in return. Teen boys are the most susceptible to this tactic.
- A good way to lessen your risk of sextortion is to never send explicit or even semiexplicit images to anyone and never open attachments from people you don't know.

TALKING TO YOUR KIDS WHO'VE BEEN INVOLVED IN SEXTORTION

AGES 13+

Key concept

I will help you and walk with you through this!

Sample dialogue

Remember, if you have sent images to a stranger online, the predator is the one committing the crime—not you! There is help for every victim of sextortion. Let's talk about what to do in the future.

- If you receive sextortion threats, you are not alone. Tell us or your other trusted friends we have recruited to get help right away.
- Report sextortion to the police or FBI as soon as possible. We can help you do this.
- Do not send any money to the person trying to sextort you. Payment hardly ever stops the problem.

While these issues are very serious and frightening, by sharing this information with our kids we are equipping them with tools to stay safer in a sometimes dark world. Any time you talk to your kids about these topics, remind them that you are their partner in these situations. You are on their team and there to help. They don't have to navigate any of this alone.

CLOSING THOUGHTS

Not too long ago I read this quote from Mr. Rogers and it hit me so hard. He said, "What we see and hear on the screen is who we become."[3] I know you don't expect to read a quote from Mr. Rogers in a book about pornography, but think about it for a minute. Mr. Rogers spent his whole career creating good things for children to consume on television because he knew that what they were watching impacted them.

I find this quote so moving because now, fifty years after Mr. Rogers started his television show for children, there is so much on screens that is harmful for our kids to consume. In many cases we don't want them to become what they see and hear on the screen.

Friends, after reading this book you know more than ever that we need to give our kids something better than what the enemy wants to offer them. We need to give them the tools and the truth so they can choose what is best. And because you read this book (that you probably never wanted to have to read), your kids will be better equipped to do just that. I am so proud of you! There is hope of sexual health and healing for your children, and their children, and their children. Generational change is at hand because you read this book. Praise God!

When I think about what we parents can offer our kids in terms of a sexual future that is healthy and full of integrity, I often think of this passage from the book of Deuteronomy chapter 30. Moses was speaking to the children of Israel as they were about to enter the promised land. I think what he described fits so perfectly with what our kids are facing today:

This day I call the heavens and the earth as witnesses against you that I have set before you life and death, blessings and curses. Now choose life, so that you and your children may live and that you may love the LORD your God, listen to his voice, and hold fast to him. For the LORD is your life, and he will give you many years in the land he swore to give to your fathers, Abraham, Isaac and Jacob. (vv. 19–20)

Life and death.

Blessings and curses.

These are the choices that lie before our children.

May we help them choose to step into blessing and life! Because you read this book, they can take that first step with you alongside them.

God bless you.

Greta

Important Concepts

What to Know and What to Do

Use this alphabetized, topical guide as a quick reference for those moments of difficult conversation or when your child asks a question you aren't sure how to answer. You could even use it as a checklist for conversations you should have with your child before they reach the end of their teen years. While not an exhaustive list, these topics are the ones parents ask me about again and again.

ANIME

Anime is a style of cartoon drawing inspired by Japanese animation. It's characterized by characters with big eyes and expressive faces. Some anime is harmless, but some is highly sexualized and objectifies women and even girls. There's also a whole segment of anime that is pornographic.

What to know

- Anime porn is called "hentai," which is the Japanese word for "perverted." It's often considered harmless because it doesn't involve real people. People defend anime pornography by arguing, "It's pretend. It's fantasy. It's just a drawing."[1]

- Because anime is a cartoon, the consumer is less likely to feel any compassion for a suffering character because they aren't real.[2] When people consume content that does not compel them to show compassion or have empathy, this spills over into other parts of their real life.

- Anime plays heavily into the schoolgirl fantasy prevalent in pornography, and some hentai depicts child porn. This makes actual child pornography only a short step away.

- The most disturbing and frightening aspect of anime porn is that absolutely anything is possible. Because it is "just a drawing," any fantasy or fetish can be acted out. The opportunity for perversion is seemingly limitless: rape, child porn, physical abuse, murder.

What to do

- If your child is drawn to anime through shows like Pokémon, be very discerning of what other anime they consume. Don't assume all anime is harmless simply because it's a cartoon.

- Do not let your child read anime-style drawing books without previewing them. They often include sexualized female characters.

- Do not let your child search for anime characters or shows unsupervised, as it is likely they will encounter highly sexualized images and videos.

- As your child gets older, discuss the problematic and disturbing elements of anime so they can make safe, wise, and discerning choices about what to consume.

IMPORTANT CONCEPTS: WHAT TO KNOW AND WHAT TO DO

BODY IMAGE

Consuming pornography negatively impacts body image for everyone from preteens to teens to adult women and men. It's also a key factor in low self-esteem and body dissatisfaction, which can lead to eating disorders. Social media is also a contributing factor in body dissatisfaction and negative body image.

What to know

- The constant use of filters and editing tools on social media increases body dissatisfaction and low self-esteem in both men and women. Filters have contributed to what is known as Snapchat Dysmorphia, in which people want to look like their filtered image and seek out medical treatment to achieve this.[3]
- When a man or boy consumes porn, he is more likely to be critical of his partner's body[4] and his own body.
- "A 2019 study showed that women whose male partners watch pornography on a regular basis are more likely to report symptoms of an eating disorder."[5]
- Partners of pornography consumers also struggle with body dissatisfaction.

What to do

- Delay giving your kids social media for as long as possible. Their developing brains don't need access to all the edited and altered images they'll encounter.
- Give your kids old-fashioned disposable cameras or a digital camera instead of taking pictures on a phone and using the editing apps to alter their photos.

167

- As your children get older, share with them that porn use has a negative impact on the way they see their own body and the bodies of others.

DISCERNMENT AND INTUITION

Discernment is seeing things as they truly are or judging things well. *Intuition* is understanding something based on how we feel. When our kids listen to a feeling that tells them something is uncomfortable or unsafe, they're listening to their intuition. When they act on that intuition, they are practicing discernment. Christians believe that the Holy Spirit is our guide in using intuition to discern when things are good or bad, safe or dangerous.

What to know

- The sense something isn't right can be described to a child as "a yucky feeling in your tummy" or an uncomfortable feeling about being in a place, what they're watching or looking at, or being with a certain person.
- Remind your child that God has given them these feelings to keep them safe, and they can tell you when they experience them.
- As a child gets older, they can use discernment to help them decide when a movie, book, art, or even a friendship or relationship is not safe or good for them. They need to know what makes them uncomfortable or unsafe and that they can walk away.

What to do

- Begin to teach kids to listen to their body, their brain, and their heart when it tells them something doesn't feel right.

- If your child has a hard time understanding how discernment works, you can explain that it is like a superpower God gave them to help keep them safe from things and people that are bad for them.
- Don't dismiss your child's moments of discernment. Listen to them, and even if you don't feel the same way, honor their instincts as best you can so they know they can count on you as a safe place in the future.
- As your children get older, help them understand that even if something is okay for them it might be problematic for others and they can respect others' instincts.

EROTIC LITERATURE

Erotic literature is any writing, usually fiction, that includes explicit sexual content intended to arouse the reader. Much of today's erotic literature is self-published or distributed online, ensuring there are no restrictions on what can be produced.

What to know

- Erotic fiction is sometimes labeled as romance. Romance novels often contain sexually explicit content. Think of them as the soft porn version of literature.
- Both romance novels and erotic literature are largely marketed to women and teen girls. If your daughter brings home a romance novel, review it to see if it has explicit content. Romances and erotic literature are not the only books that contain sexually explicit material. All YA literature, especially more recently published titles, and all adult

novels could contain graphic sexual material. If you want to know what your child is reading, read the book yourself or find a trusted source for book recommendations.

- Mildly explicit content can build an appetite for more explicit and pornographic content. Many teen girls and women trace their pornography use and addiction to reading romance novels and then moving on to erotic literature and porn use.
- If your child is reading any kind of romance or erotic literature online, be aware that it is often the most explicit and extreme content available, and they will be exposed to dangerous and highly objectionable material.

What to do

- Use discernment before letting your child read romance novels and use extreme caution before letting them read romance novels with mildly explicit sexual content. Absolutely do not let them read erotic literature, as it is pornography on a page.
- As your child gets older, discuss the problematic and disturbing elements of romance novels and erotic literature so they can make safe, wise, and discerning choices about what types of literature they consume.

GROOMING

Grooming is when someone builds a relationship and emotional connection with a child or young person to abuse, exploit, or even traffic them. A groomer can be a man or a woman of any age, and grooming can happen over a short period of time or over years. Groomers might manipulate a child by threatening their family or threatening to expose the child. For adolescents, they might give compliments and pretend to have an innocent crush. Once a relationship is established, the predator might ask for explicit photos or videos or even suggest a face-to-face meetup. Young teens are often the most at risk but all children are susceptible.

What to know

- Both boys and girls can be targets for online predators.
- Predatory behavior (sometimes called online enticement) starts off seeming innocent by being friendly, complimentary, or helpful. The National Center for Missing and Exploited Children saw a 97.5 percent increase in reports of online enticement from 2019 to 2020. And the numbers continue to go up.[6]
- Grooming can take place in person or online.
- If in person, the groomer is almost always someone in a position of authority or trust.
- Online groomers often hide their identity and age by pretending to be someone of the opposite gender or close in age to the child.
- Grooming can take place through social media apps, online video games, messenger apps, email, or texting. You must know who your child is communicating with online!
- Showing a child pornography or exposing them to other sexualized material can be a grooming tool for sexual abuse.
- Children can feel loyalty or friendship toward the groomer even if they also feel fear and distress over the relationship.

- Signs that your child is being groomed might be changes in their mood like anger, depression, sadness, or anxiety.
- Take notice if your child has trouble sleeping, becomes secretive, or has new gifts that can't be explained.
- If your child has sexual questions or is acting out sexually, these could be signs of sexual abuse.

What to do

- Talk to your children about online predators. Explain what they are, what they do, and how your child should respond if a stranger approaches them online.
- If your child is playing video games online where they are playing with strangers (or even friends), have them play in a public part of the house without headphones so it's harder for them to hide conversations and messages.
- Remind your child repeatedly that they can talk to you if they encounter anyone who makes them feel uncomfortable or uneasy.
- If your child exhibits any concerning behaviors, take a close look at their online activity as well as their in-person relationships.
- If your child confesses that they've been abused or are in an abusive relationship, tell them they are safe with you and not in trouble.
- Do not talk to the accused abuser. Instead, report what the child has told you right away to the appropriate authorities: the police, child protective services, or a child abuse hotline.
- If abuse of any kind has occurred, get the child to a counselor trained to deal with this kind of trauma.

MEDIA LITERACY

See chapter 5, "Why You Have to Learn to Discern."

MINOR-ATTRACTED PERSONS

Minor-attracted persons, sometimes called MAPs, are people who are sexually attracted to minors. The correct term is "pedophile," but the term "minor-attracted person" has been adopted more recently, as there is a growing movement to portray these people as victims because they are often rejected by society.

What to know

- A popular genre in pornography is called "barely legal"— images or movies of people who look or may be underage. One of the top searches at Porn Hub year after year is "teen."[7]
- Teens need to be aware of the growing trend to rebrand pedophilia as MAPs.
- A Google search leads to articles portraying MAPs as victims. Teens need to be able to identify this as a false and dangerous narrative.
- Teens also need to know that consuming porn shapes the viewer's sexual appetite and rewires the brain, making things that once seemed inappropriate or unethical now seem arousing.[8]

What to do

- Tell your teens the truth about MAPs, even if it makes you uncomfortable.

- Help your teens use critical thinking skills and media literacy tools by pulling up articles on MAPs and letting them read and talk about them with you.
- Talk to your older teen about how porn consumers can become desensitized to traditional porn and begin to desire other genres that are even more destructive.
- Remind your teens to talk to you if they see or learn about someone using teen or barely legal porn, as it can lead to even more dangerous things like child sexual abuse material.

ONLINE PREDATORS

See *Grooming* and chapter 14, "How Do I Talk About Sexting, Nudes, and Sextortion with My Kids?"

POP-UP ADS

Pop-up ads will appear on a website to persuade the viewer to click on them. Cyber criminals use them to get personal information through phishing scams or malware. They can also expose kids to positive impressions of alcohol, vaping, and marijuana use and invite unsuspecting kids to keep clicking through until they are exposed to soft porn images or even porn sites.

What to know

- Nearly all games, apps, and videos—even for very young children—contain pop-up ads.

- Many pop-up ads contain a video game–like element, making them even more enticing to click on.
- Even in an app or game designated for younger children, there is no guarantee that the pop-up ad will be age appropriate.

What to do

- Instruct your younger children never to click on a pop-up ad. If they are interested in it, they can show you and ask you to help them.
- When your children are older and can make decisions about online behavior on their own, make sure you have explained the dangers that are associated with pop-up ads. Encourage them to make it a practice to avoid using them.

PORNIFIED CULTURE

See chapter 5, "Why You Have to Learn to Discern."

PUBERTY

Puberty is when a child's body begins to physically mature into an adult's body capable of sexual reproduction. Hormones drive these changes, which happen over the course of several years. Puberty typically begins between the ages of ten and fourteen, but it can also start earlier or later. Emotional changes also occur: A child might feel more easily angered or irritated, feel sadder than they used to, or experience more up-and-down moods.

They'll probably become more interested in their looks and want more privacy in general.

What to know

- Puberty does not mean your sweet baby is gone forever. Your child still needs you to love them and hug them and show affection, even if they appear uncomfortable.
- Your child's peers are probably experiencing the same changes and might be discussing them. Strive to be the number one source of information around puberty, body changes, sex, etc.
- If you use a book, video series, or curriculum to talk to your kids about puberty or sex, preview the resource before sharing it with your kid. Not all will uphold your values.

What to do

- Don't treat puberty—or your child who is going through it—like a horrible disease. It's a time full of new and different and sometimes challenging things, but it is also what allows them to become adults and have a family. That is a gift!
- Be extra gentle and kind with your child as they go through puberty. Offer them things like more time alone, taking a hot bath, or having a cup of tea when they are moody; making them a favorite meal; or taking them out with you to give them space from siblings.
- Sympathize with them when it feels like their hormones are going crazy; you know what that is like.
- If you haven't talked to your child about sex, the onset of puberty is a good time to begin those conversations.
- Other topics to cover as your child goes through puberty are body odor, acne, penis size and breast size, erections and wet

dreams, masturbation, vaginal discharge, nutrition and exercise, and menstruation. These don't need to be covered all at once, but they should be brought up over time or as needed.

- Your sons should know that a girl on her period is not a mean or crazy person, and her period isn't something embarrassing. Teach him how to support a girl or woman on her period, including having knowledge of the supplies she might need.

SAFE PHONES

Safe phones are phones without (or with limited) internet or access to apps, gaming, and social media. Some have cameras or offer access to music, but mostly safe phones exist for calling and texting. Sometimes they have a touch screen, but others are the old-fashioned flip phones many of us remember.

What to know
- The sooner a child gets a smartphone, the sooner they become attached and face all the troubles that come with it.
- More and more companies are making great safe phones. If your child needs a phone to get in touch with you, a safe phone is a great option. They're also a good way for kids to learn how to use a phone wisely and practice good phone etiquette.

What to do
- Consider delaying any kind of phone for your child as long as possible.
- Once your child has reached a time (not an age) when having a phone is necessary, start them off with a safe phone.

- Make sure the child knows it is a family phone, and everyone has access to it.
- Teach them safe texting and calling practices, including managing their time on it.
- When your child needs a phone with internet capabilities, make the transition to a smartphone. I suggest age sixteen or older.

SEX ADDICTION

A person who has a sex addiction has a compulsive need to be sexually stimulated, sometimes multiple times a day. Sex addiction can manifest as consuming pornography, masturbation, sexting, prostitution, and affairs. This can include risky, destructive, or dangerous behaviors and interfere with work, friendships, school, finances, and a regular enjoyment of life.

What to know

- The number of teens experiencing sexual addiction is growing steadily.
- A common thread for people with sex addiction is exposure to porn or some kind of sexual abuse at a young age followed by no help or support to recover from that experience.
- Warning signs of sex addiction include
  - spending more time alone,
  - feeling anxious or irritable or depressed,
  - being secretive or lying about time spent online or with people,
  - isolating from activities or people that used to bring joy,

- o problems at school or work, and
- o making poor decisions.
- Effects of sex addiction include
  - o struggling with poor self-image or self-esteem,
  - o inability to form real connections with friends and romantic partners,
  - o intimacy disorders,
  - o lack of impulse control, and
  - o struggles in regular social situations.

What to do

- If you notice any of these behaviors in your teen, take a look at all their online activity. This could be challenging if they are swiping out their online history or hiding it from you, and there is a strong chance they'll feel you have violated their privacy. But if there is a problem, or even the hint of a problem, it is far better to address it and get help.
- The best-case scenario is to help your child avoid negative sexual exposure or behavior from the beginning by providing layers of protection (see chapters 6 and 7).
- If you notice worrisome behavior or discover signs of troubling sexual behavior, seek help (see the Resource Guide at the end of this book).

SEX TRAFFICKING

Sex trafficking is using force, extortion, coercion, or fraud to get someone to engage in commercial sex acts against their will. If the case involves a minor, it is considered human trafficking even if coercion or extortion are not explicitly involved. Increasingly, victims are being trafficked by their own family members or other people they know. "The Human Trafficking Hotline identifies pornography as the top-ranked industry for sex trafficking."[9]

According to the US Department of Justice, "No child is immune to becoming a victim . . . Individuals can now use websites and social media to advertise, schedule, and purchase sexual encounters with minors."[10]

What to know

- Anyone can be at risk for sex trafficking, though some people and populations—including youth and children—are more vulnerable.
- There is no such thing as "ethical porn." "Nearly half of sex trafficking victims report that pornography was made of them while they were in bondage."[11]
- By consuming pornography there is a strong possibility that a person is participating in sex trafficking.

What to do

- Explain to your teen the definition of sex trafficking so they know the dangers and warning signs.
- Remind them that viewing pornography can contribute to sex trafficking and further exploit the victims.
- Ask your teen if they've heard people justify porn by saying they use only "ethical porn." Remind them that there's no way to verify that no one was being coerced or exploited in producing porn.

SEXUAL VIOLENCE IN PORNOGRAPHY

If you read or research the pornography currently being produced, you'll learn about violent porn, which is no longer the exception but the rule. A 2019 study found that of the fifty most popular porn videos, 88 percent contained violence.[12]

What to know

- In the vast majority of cases, the recipients of violence in porn were women.
- More youth are using porn as their sex education and therefore accept violence as a normal part of sexual encounters.
- When porn and violence are connected, it eroticizes violence, making it seem sexy and desirable, especially to the one perpetrating the violence.
- Adolescent boys are particularly susceptible to internalizing this because it puts the male in a place of power and authority.
- Adolescent girls either find the prospect of sex terrifying because of the violent acts or they accept that as what their partners want.

What to do

- Talk to your teen about violent porn. Explain that violence should play no part in a sexual encounter or relationship. Remind them that porn dehumanizes people, which makes it easier to abuse them.
- Make sure your teen knows that porn provides a false and distorted view of sex, and it is not the place to learn about sex.

- If your teen has questions or wants to know more about sex, they need to come to you. If they are too embarrassed to do that, find a trusted adult they can talk to or give them a book that you have vetted.
- Make sure your sons know that violence against women should never be tolerated, even if they hear that is what girls want or what they have seen in porn.
- Make sure your daughters know that violence against women should never be tolerated, and if any man makes her feel unsafe she has every right to walk away immediately.

Scripts to Use with Your Kids

Resource Guide

BOOKS

Pornography and Body Safety (Read with Your Kids)

God Made All of Me: A Book to Help Children Protect Their Bodies by Justin and Lindsey Holcomb (ages 4–10)

Good Pictures Bad Pictures Jr.: A Simple Plan to Protect Young Minds by Kristen Jenson (ages 5–8)

Good Pictures Bad Pictures: Porn Proofing Today's Young Kids by Kristen Jenson (ages 9–12)

How to Talk to Your Kids About Pornography by Dina Alexander (ages 12 and up)

Shout NO!: A Child's Rhyme About Tricky People . . . and What to Do by Sara Ernst (ages 3–6)

Healthy Sexuality (Read with Your Kids)

Chasing Love: Sex, Love, and Relationships in a Confused Culture by Sean McDowell (read with your teen)

God Made Babies: Helping Parents Answer the Baby Question by Justin and Lindsey Holcomb (ages 4–10)

God Made Me in His Image: Helping Children Appreciate Their Bodies by Justin and Lindsey Holcomb (ages 4–10)

Outdated: Find Love That Lasts When Dating Has Changed by
Jonathan Pokluda (read and discuss with your older teen)
A Student's Guide to Culture by John Stonestreet and Brett
Kunkle (read with your teen)

Pornography (for Adults)

Fight for Love: How to Take Your Marriage Back from Porn
by Rosie Makinney
*Her Freedom Journey: A Guide Out of Porn and Shame to
Authentic Intimacy* by Julie Slattery and Joy Skarka
*The Porn Myth: Exploring the Reality Behind the Fantasy of
Pornography* by Matt Fradd
*Protecting Your Children from Internet Pornography:
Understanding the Science, Risks, and Ways to Protect
Your Kids* by John D. Foubert

Healthy Sexuality (for Adults)

*Behind Closed Doors: A Guide to Help Parents and Teens
Navigate Through Life's Toughest Issues* by Jessica L. Peck
*Free to Thrive: How Your Hurt, Struggles, and Deepest
Longings Can Lead to a Fulfilling Life* by Josh McDowell
and Ben Bennett
*Honest Talk: A New Perspective on Talking to Your Kids
About Sex* by John W. Fort
Rethinking Sexuality: God's Design and Why It Matters by
Dr. Juli Slattery

Healthy Tech Use

*The Anxious Generation: How the Great Rewiring of Childhood
Is Causing an Epidemic of Mental Illness* by Jonathan Haidt

*Creating a Tech-Healthy Family: Ten Must-Have
    Conversations to Help You Worry Less and Connect
    More with Your Kids* by Andrea Davis
*The Opt-Out Family: How to Give Your Kids What
    Technology Can't* by Erin Loechner
*The Tech-Wise Family: Everyday Steps for Putting
    Technology in Its Proper Place* by Andy Crouch

WEBSITES

Information on Pornography

Fight the New Drug: www.fightthenewdrug.org
Josh McDowell Ministry: www.josh.org

Tools for Protecting Kids and Tech Safety

Cyber Safety Cop: www.cybersafetycop.com
Greta Eskridge: www.gretaeskridge.com
Protect Young Eyes: www.protectyoungeyes.com

Pornography and Sex Addiction Recovery

Beggar's Daughter: https://beggarsdaughter.com
Fight For Love Ministries: www.fightforloveministries.org
Pure Desire Ministries: www.puredesire.org
Relativity: www.sexualrecovery.com
SheRecovery: https://sherecovery.com

Child Sexual Exploitation and Sex Trafficking

Child Rescue Coalition: www.childrescuecoalition.org
Enough Is Enough: www.enough.org

Exodus Cry: www.exoduscry.com

International Justice Mission: www.ijm.org

Healthy Sexuality and Conversations at Home

Birds and Bees and Kids: www.birdsandbeesandkids.com

Sex Ed Reclaimed: www.sexedreclaimed.com

SOFTWARE AND APPS

Bark: www.bark.us

Canopy: www.getcanopy.com

Covenant Eyes: www.covenanteyes.com

Kaspersky Safe Kids: www.kaspersky.com/safe-kids

Net Nanny: www.netnanny.com

SAFE PHONES

Bark: www.bark.us

Gabb: https://gabb.com

Pinwheel: www.pinwheel.com

Troomi: https://troomi.com

Acknowledgments

This book was never a book I wanted to write, but I knew I had to. And now I'm so glad I did. From that fateful day when I thought my whole world was coming to an end until now, I have prayed that God would use my family's story to bring hope and healing to others. There were times when that was almost impossible to imagine. But God and his people have been faithful, and this book is evidence of that. So this is my attempt to convey my most heartfelt thanks for the many who have helped us get here.

To Aaron, thank you for your dedication and determination to heal and to love me more deeply and truly every day. Thank you for courageously saying yes to this book and all the things before it. Thank you for pouring hope and love into others who are hurting. I admire you. I love you so much.

To James, William, Lilly, and Davy, thank you for putting up with a mom who talks about porn. A lot. You all have been so gracious, even though I know it's been awkward and probably kind of weird sometimes. Thank you for telling me you are proud of me. That means more to me than I could say.

To all the ones who stood by us and with us in the darkest days: Jim, Jason and Erin, Cathy, Greg and Jana, Jessica, Betsy. We owe you such a debt of gratitude and will never forget your love.

To Josh McDowell, thank you for bravely sharing your story and helping me share mine.

To Forest Home, thank you for providing a place for us to heal and grow and begin to share our story. We are forever grateful for the impact you've had on our whole family.

To the *At Home Podcast* girls, thank you for letting me do that first podcast on porn, even though it was wildly awkward and uncomfortable, and I was so incredibly nervous. You gave me a place to start sharing.

To each of you who listened, encouraged, and prayed for me in the years it took for this book to come to be: Anjuli, Leah, Megan, Karen, Dianne, Rea, Ali, Brook, Emily, Elizabeth, Deb, Sally, Chris, Rosie, Ginny, Emilie, Cat, Elsie. Every time I see this book, I think of you. Your friendship means so very much to me.

To my agent, Jenni Burke, thank you for being my partner and my guide. Thank you for believing in this book and in me from the beginning. I am deeply grateful for you.

To my editor, Brigitta Nortker, thank you for shepherding this book and shepherding me as I wrote it. You were a counselor and a friend, and this book is here and better because of you. I appreciate you so very much.

And lastly, to each one of you who has supported me over the years, attended my seminars, asked me to speak in your churches, and been on my team, thank you! I wrote this book for you and your kids. Together we can give them something better!

Notes

A Letter to Parents

1. Elisabeth Elliot, *These Strange Ashes* (1975; repr., Revell, 2023), 12.
2. Kaylena Radcliff, "A War Story: 'There Is No Pit So Deep God's Love Is Not Deeper Still,'" *Christian History* no. 121 (2017), https://christianhistoryinstitute.org/magazine/article/there-is-no-pit-so-deep.

One: Why I Became an Unlikely Porn Fighter

1. Gabriela Coca and Jocelyn Wikle, "What Happens When Children Are Exposed to Pornography," Institute for Family Studies, April 30, 2024, https://ifstudies.org/blog/what-happens-when-children-are-exposed-to-pornography, quoting from Common Sense Media, *Teens and Pornography*, January 10, 2023, https://www.commonsensemedia.org/research/teens-and-pornography.
2. Quoted in Matt Fradd, *The Porn Myth: Exposing the Reality Behind the Fantasy of Pornography* (Ignatius Press, 2017), 57.
3. "Internet Pornography by the Numbers; A Significant Threat to Society," Webroot, accessed August 12, 2024, https://www.webroot.com/us/en/resources/tips-articles/internet-pornography-by-the-numbers.

Two: Why Moms Need to Break the Silence

1. Fradd, *Porn Myth*, 194.
2. Catherine Marshall, *Christy* (1967; repr., Evergreen Farm, 2017), 95.

Three: Why Your Kids Need to Hear You Talk About Porn

1. Kristin MacLaughlin, "The Detrimental Effects of Pornography on Small Children," Net Nanny, December 19, 2017, https://www .netnanny.com/blog/the-detrimental-effects-of-pornography -on-small-children.

Four: Why You Need to Parent from a Place of Hope

1. Daniel Weiss and Joshua Glaser, *Treading Boldly Through a Pornographic World: A Field Guide for Parents* (Salem Books, 2021), 13–14.

Five: Why You Have to Learn to Discern

1. Alexander Eser, "Global Pornography Industry Statistics: $97 Billion Revenue, Shocking Consumption Trends," World Metrics, July 23, 2024, https://worldmetrics.org/pornography -industry-statistics/.
2. "Kraft Mac & Cheese Encourages You to Send Noods to Friends and Family," Kraft Heinz Company, October 6, 2020, https:// news.kraftheinzcompany.com/press-releases-details/2020/Kraft -Mac--Cheese-Encourages-You-to-Send-Noods-to-Friends-and -Family/default.aspx.
3. Aly Walansky, "Kraft Removes 'Send Noods' Campaign After Backlash: 'Listen to All These Moms!!,'" TODAY, October 13, 2020, https://www.today.com/food/kraft-axes-send-noods -campaign-after-social-media-uproar-t194370.
4. John Stonestreet and Brett Kunkle, *A Student's Guide to Culture* (David C Cook, 2020), 76.
5. Stonestreet and Kunkle, *Student's Guide to Culture*, 76.

Six: Create a Healthy Sexual Culture in Your Home

1. Greta Eskridge, host, *The Greta Eskridge Podcast*, podcast, "We Have a Good Story to Tell! Talking to Your Kids About Sex— with Megan Michelson," April 23, 2024,

https://www.christianparenting.org/podcast/the-greta-eskridge
-podcast/we-have-a-good-story-to-tell-talking-to-your-kids
-about-sex-with-megan-michelson.

Eight: Respond with Compassion Instead of Judgment

1. Juli Slattery, *Rethinking Sexuality: God's Design and Why It Matters* (Multnomah, 2018), 26.
2. C. S. Lewis, *The Weight of Glory* (1941; repr., HarperOne, 2001), 182.

Nine: Walk a Different Path

1. Safe phones are phones that look and function like regular smartphones but don't have internet access or social media. Some have safety features that notify parents if troubling messages or images come through texts. Ultimately these phones solve the problem of parents wanting to be able to contact their kid or vice versa without handing them a fully loaded smartphone. Some companies that make safe phones are Gabb, Bark, Pinwheel, and Troomi (see the Resource Guide for more information).

Ten: Pursue Connection with Your Kids

1. Fradd, *Porn Myth*, 150.
2. Naomi Wolf, "The Porn Myth," *New York Magazine*, October 9, 2003, https://nymag.com/nymetro/news/trends/n_9437/.
3. Michaeleen Doucleff, "The Truth About Teens, Social Media and the Mental Health Crisis," NPR, April 25, 2023, https://www.npr.org/sections/health-shots/2023/04/25/1171773181/social-media-teens-mental-health.

Twelve: How Do I Talk About Masturbation with My Kids?

1. John W. Fort, *Honest Talk: A New Perspective on Talking to Your Kids About Sex* (Be Broken, 2019), 122.
2. Fort, *Honest Talk*, 119.

Fourteen: How Do I Talk About Sexting, Nudes, and Sextortion with My Kids?

1. "What Is Sextortion?," Federal Bureau of Investigation, accessed September 6, 2024, https://www.fbi.gov/video-repository/what -is-sextortion/view.
2. Emma Henderson Vaughan, "NCMEC Releases New Sextortion Data," National Center for Missing and Exploited Children, April 15, 2024, https://www.missingkids.org/blog/2024/ncmec -releases-new-sextortion-data.
3. Attributed to Fred Rogers at Kira Zizzo, "Movie Tells Story of a Good Man," *Colorado Kids*, June 19, 2018, https://nieonline.com /coloradonie/downloads/coloradokids/CK061918b.pdf.

Important Concepts: What to Know and What to Do

1. Fradd, *Porn Myth*, 130.
2. Fradd, 131.
3. Traci Pedersen, "How Does Social Media Affect Body Image?," PsychCentral, updated on February 27, 2023, https://psychcentral .com/health/how-the-media-affects-body-image.
4. Madeleine McElligott, "Pornography, Negative Body Image, & Eating Disorders: The Connections," National Center on Sexual Exploitation, February 27, 2023, https://endsexualexploitation.org /articles/pornography-negative-body-image-eating-disorders-the -connections/.
5. McElligott, "Pornography, Negative Body Image, & Eating Disorders."
6. "Online Enticement," National Center for Missing and Exploited Children, accessed September 6, 2024, https://www.missingkids .org/netsmartz/topics/onlineenticement.
7. "'Teen': Why Has This Porn Category Topped the Charts for 6+ Years?," Fight the New Drug, accessed September 6, 2024, https:// fightthenewdrug.org/this-years-most-popular-genre-of-porn -is-pretty-messed-up/.
8. "'Teen': Why Has This Porn Category Topped the Charts for 6+ Years?," Fight the New Drug.

9. "Pornography and Human Trafficking," The Asservo Project, September 27, 2022, https://www.theasservoproject.org/pornography -and-human-trafficking/.
10. "Child Sex Trafficking," US Department of Justice: Criminal Division, updated September 20, 2023, https://www.justice.gov /criminal/criminal-ceos/child-sex-trafficking.
11. "The Link Between Pornography and Human Trafficking," Dressember, accessed September 6, 2024, https://www.dressember .org/blog/thepornographylink.
12. Priyanka Vasavan, "The Sex Industry, Pornography, Violence," *The Daily Cardinal*, March 2, 2023, https://www.dailycardinal .com/article/2023/03/the-sex-industry-pornography-violence.

9. "Pornography and Human Trafficking," Fight the New Drug, Fight the New Drug, accessed September 27, 2021, https://www.fightthenewdrug.org/pornography-and-human-trafficking.

10. J. Child Sex. Traffic. Abus., US Department of Justice, Criminal Division, updated September 20, 2022, https://www.justice.gov/criminal-ceos/child-sex-trafficking.

11. "The Link Between Pornography and Human Trafficking," Dressember, accessed September 6, 2021, https://www.dressember.org/blog/the-pornography-link.

12. Priyanka Runwal, "The Sex Industry: Pornography Violence," The Guardian, March 2, 2022, https://www.theguardian.com/global-development/2022/mar/02/the-sex-industry-pornography-violence.

About the Author

Greta Eskridge is a second-generation homeschooling mom to four and wife of twenty-six years to Aaron. She's also the author of *Adventuring Together* and *100 Days of Adventure* and the host of the popular *Greta Eskridge Podcast*. She loves nature, books, and coffee. Greta is passionate about helping families create connection, preserve childhood, and chase adventure.

Also available from Greta Eskridge

Adventuring Together: How to Create Connections and Make Lasting Memories With Your Kids

100 Days of Adventure: Nature Activities, Creative Projects, and Field Trips for Every Season

AVAILABLE WHEREVER BOOKS ARE SOLD.

Connect with Greta

THE GRETA ESKRIDGE PODCAST
Available on your favorite podcast app

INSTAGRAM
Follow Greta at @maandpamodern

WEBSITE
GretaEskridge.com